ADVANCE PRAISE

"This outstanding book is a crystal-clear analysis of how and why higher education got captured by the finance industry. It's also the definitive guide for those who want to free themselves and their institutions from the sticky trap set by Wall Street."
—**Andrew Ross**, author of *Creditocracy: And the Case for Debt Refusal*

"Institutional debt is used to push the rising cost of public college education onto students and their families—predominantly Black, Brown, and white working class—while enriching Wall Street and the wealthy. It's a textbook case of racialized austerity imposed on an increasingly diverse student population, the effect of which is public colleges and universities that are beholden to bondholders and credit rating agencies, not to the public. It does not have to be this way.

In *Lend & Rule*, the Coalition Against Campus Debt takes on the corporatization of higher ed and makes a definitive case for the urgent role of public higher ed workers' unions to lead—and win. It is a call for action for workers, students, and the public to fight against racial capitalism and for free public education for all."
—**Rotua Lumbantobing**, Associate Professor of Business at Western Connecticut State University and Vice President of American Association of University Professors

"*Lend & Rule* is the book that university students and workers have been waiting for. It offers a cutting analysis of how institutional debt makes campus jobs worse and how debt erodes the public mission of education by filling the pockets of financiers with tuition dollars from the nation's most exploited students. More than that, *Lend & Rule* offers a positive vision of how to organize against this status quo and make necessary change towards a truly democratic higher education system."
—**Andy Hines**, author of *Outside Literary Studies: Black Criticism and the University* and the editor of *University Keywords*

T0286207

"*Lend & Rule* is a shocking exposé of the debt crisis no one is talking about. Our colleges and universities are buried in institutional debt, with dire consequences for all of us. This dynamite book shows how to look under the financial hood so we can build well-informed movements with the power to win real change. A must read for everyone who cares about higher education."
—**Astra Taylor,** author of *The Age of Insecurity: Coming Together as Things Fall Apart*

"As a teacher and union leader that bargains with the third largest school district on behalf of half a million students and thirty thousand educators, I know first hand how big banks manipulate school budgets to gain profits at the expense of our students and classrooms. In *Lend & Rule*, we hear from visionaries in our movement who show us that a different system is possible, one that allows us to grow and develop ourselves and our communities in ways that won't result in the immiseration of the many for the benefit of the few. The book also shows how debt is weaponized and racialized to harm the most marginalized in our society, but when we come together to tax the rich and collectivize our institutions, we can provide the public services and accommodations that we all deserve—for free."
—**Jackson Potter**, Chicago Teachers' Union

"*Lend & Rule* provides labor organizers, workers, and students in higher education the theoretical analysis and organizing tools we need to transform our public higher education system. Revealing how the 'shadow governance' of financial capitalism works, this book opens up new terrains of struggle for education justice."
—**Todd Wolfson**, Associate Professor of Media Studies at Rutgers University and President of American Association of University Professors

"*Lend & Rule* is simultaneously a fantastic deep dive into a core truth, that private finance, free markets, and market competition are incapable of providing a basic public good; and an organizing manual for all those committed to protecting and expanding access to higher education."
—**Donald Cohen**, Executive Director of In the Public Interest

LEND & RULE

LEND & RULE

FIGHTING THE SHADOW FINANCIALIZATION OF PUBLIC UNIVERSITIES

The Coalition Against
Campus Debt

Philadelphia, PA
Brooklyn, NY
commonnotions.org

ISBN: 978-1-945335-12-9 | eBook ISBN: 978-1-945335-25-9
Library of Congress Number: 2024941243

10 9 8 7 6 5 4 3 2 1

Common Notions   Common Notions
c/o Interference Archive   c/o Making Worlds Bookstore
314 7th St.   210 S. 45th St.
Brooklyn, NY 11215   Philadelphia, PA 19104

www.commonnotions.org
info@commonnotions.org

Discounted bulk quantities of our books are available for organizing, educational, or fundraising purposes. Please contact Common Notions at the address above for more information.

Cover design by Josh MacPhee
Layout design and typesetting by Suba Murugan
Printed by union labor in Canada on acid-free paper

CONTENTS

Appendix

INTRODUCTION
HOW WE GOT HERE

This book is the product of collective inquiry, analysis, action, and reflection. We—faculty, staff, organizers, union leaders, and union members— came together during a pandemic to make sense of the world shaping our choices and determine how we could instead shape the world. The first seeds of this inquiry came from conversations in the Public Higher Education Workers (PHEW) network, a collective of union members across US campuses attempting to transform and democratize their unions. When the pandemic hit, the group swelled as higher education workers looked for ways to make sense of the crisis and organize within it.

At the beginning of the COVID-19 pandemic lockdowns in Spring 2020, many of us held hope that the pause in the status quo—a disruption to the drumbeat of daily affairs—would open what Arundhati Roy calls a portal of transition between possible worlds. We began to imagine the university we wanted and needed on the other side of the portal: a space of liberation, imagination, resistance, and democratic practice. We drew up outlines of the university we wanted and brought workers, students, and community members into conversations to name and claim this vision. Yet, we were often stymied in organizing toward this vision since workers were isolated in space and time by the remote work dominating many campuses. Our hope that a collective response to the virus would bring us together waned as government responses maintained the circulation of capital, not the collective well-being, and shaped pandemic responses into individual decisions.

Nevertheless, we continued to name our vision for the public university and dug deeper into why this vision was seemingly so out of reach. We all understood that decades of cuts to public higher education funding under demands for austerity (a funding policy committed to reducing taxes by cutting costs at public institutions) were bleeding our campuses of full-time faculty and staff and increasing students' tuition, fees, and debt. However, we did not realize how the state's withdrawal from funding left room for financiers to move in and remake the university by controlling its debt.

Our inquiry into institutional debt began as we lamented the paucity of funding for higher education and one of us (likely Jason or Eleni, who were both connected to the Debt Collective) said something like, "Yeah, and they make up for the absence of funds by taking on debt." And so our search began: how much debt? Who decides? How is debt impacting students and the resources available for teaching and research? How does debt impact the decision-making, priorities, purpose, and vision of the university?

This book introduces what we have ascertained and the organizing we have accomplished. Our attempts to make sense of debt and develop a strategy to expose and dismantle it are rooted in class struggle unionism (i.e., workers' power to name their world, envision a more just world, and organize collectively to win that world). Despite the fog surrounding institutional debt, we are committed to the conviction that workers (and students) can understand how debt works and how it undermines their institutions. We pursued a Freirean model of organizing around campus debt that invited workers to identify how debt financing operated on their campus and to what effect. We held webinars to help participants throw off the burdens of debt shame and imagine a world without debt. Eventually, we developed a generalized system for investigating campus debt (Appendix B). This organizing connected campus workers across the country through sponsored debt reveal days. These pages invite others into this work to educate ourselves, refuse the world as given, and make demands for the world we want.

DEBT, CAPITAL, AND THE PUBLIC GOOD

We enter this discussion refusing the naturalization of debt. Debt—whether student debt, medical debt, or other debt relative to meeting basic human needs—is a manifestation of a society that does not provide for people. The act of naturalizing debt obscures both how debt (both personal and institutional) operates as a mechanism of control and how we can create a new world that provides for our needs. This is to say, our critique of institutional debt in public higher education emerges from a critique of capitalism.

Within capitalism, debt is a lien on one's time—present and future. In order to pay our debts, we are required to sell our labor. This binds our time, locking us between the demands of employers and those of the banks. Perhaps the best evidence of this was the human freedom generated by the student debt payment moratorium during the COVID-19 pandemic. Without having to pay their loans, people simply did not work as much. They reclaimed their time—their lives—as theirs.

The debt economy reflects the commodification of basic needs and the individualization of providing for necessities. It exploits workers, whose insufficient wages cannot meet their needs for schooling, health, and housing (among other needs of daily life). While one set of capitalists robs our time through the exploitation of our labor, another set squeezes us through interest payments, garnering wages, and limiting our capacity to enjoy whatever meager gains we are able to claim.

Our goal, therefore, is not to create a more equitable and somewhat less restrictive debt economy. We seek to end the reliance on debt, to free both individuals and public institutions through collective support. We recognize the utopian elements of this vision but insist on holding to a horizon in which debt is abolished, even as the path toward that vision might be marked by contradictions and half-measures.

In the context of public higher education, these contradictions emerge relative to what constitutes "public" within capitalism. What does it mean to make demands for *public* funding, when *public* currently means state control, and the state itself is controlled by capitalist and, in some cases, fascist forces? Institutions of higher education have produced and reproduced systems of oppression for centuries. They have restricted access, promulgated theory and research to reify the status quo, and raised the few above the many. At the same time, public higher education has been a space of resistance and creativity. In the heyday of free public higher education at institutions like the City University of New York and the California State University system, classrooms were filled with students from working-class homes (many of them first and second-generation immigrants). The civil rights movement opened the (free) university's doors to Black and Puerto Rican students, creating the potential for a divided working class to unite.

The defunding of public higher education (and the increasing reliance on debt for funding) began in earnest just as doors were opened for Black and Brown students. This was not coincidental. As we show in the following pages, the debt economy operates within racial capitalism, where racial identity marks some for intensified systemic exploitation. From access to housing and health-care, to the repressive forces of the police state and the deliberate underfunding of public education for and in communities of color, the ravages of capitalism extract a particular toll on people of color. In this way, capitalism exploits racial identities to further divide working people. Just as we must name and refuse the naturalization of debt, we must name and refuse the racism that deepens exploitation and division. This is central to our project.

In the immediate short term, our demands insist on the state fully funding free public higher education. This would begin to release the claims of debt on students and institutions. But this is not without its contradictions. Our efforts to unbind people and public institutions from debt are one piece of dismantling the larger system of racial capitalism, which infects our social and economic relations. However, the state, under racial capitalism, does not share our interest in education as a site of liberation. The liberatory practice we aim for requires participatory democracy both within and outside of the university. Our horizon looks to state funding supported by a deeply democratic process of imagining the public university that eschews the many ways our relations and imaginations are bound by capital. Indeed, our focus on public higher education emerges, in part, from our commitment to reclaiming the commons and democratizing the public good. Our vision for public higher education within a socialist project can—and must—be prefigured in classrooms and union halls. For now, we live within the contradiction of fighting for funding from a state that attempts to bind our practice.

OUR VISION FOR PUBLIC UNIVERSITIES AND COLLEGES

As organizers, we understand the need to go beyond naming what we are fighting against. We must also name what we are fighting for. In naming what could be, we invite others into a knowledge of the possible that highlights the disparities between what we have and what we need.

We envision public universities as:

Sites not merely to learn practical skills and how to accept/get by in existing society but to challenge the roots of existing society and learn why and how to revolutionize it for the better.

Protected sites where anticapitalist ways of being and relating can be experienced, developed, prefigured, and incubated since public universities already hold latent possibilities of the commons—the very nature of classrooms allows for reimagining our social relations.

Sites to learn community. They should be spaces to explore passions and skills and how to apply them to make a meaningful life; to meet with and confront the world in as many ways as possible, including cultivating new anticapitalist, antiracist, etc. social relations that allow new ways to know ourselves.

Sites of resistance, refuge, liberation, revolution, and hope that are rooted in society and foster dreams of better possible worlds.

Sites for a community of learners and creators who, by way of conversation and reflection, question what they know and ways of knowing and work together to improve their communities.

Sites for envisioning and becoming more than we currently are. Where we can begin to see/uncover/experience possibilities for the world and for humanity—the time, the space, and the provocation to imagine and engage with others.

Paraphrasing Marx, we can think of freedom as the ability to develop potentiality as an end in itself. Thus, public universities should similarly be a time-space for such collective cultivation of human potentiality. A place to delegitimize oppression and foster/nurture more just ways of being in the world. A place where we learn how to ethically respond to one another and ourselves. This vision sees the public university as "in common" space open and accessible to all, for the good of all.

SPECIFICALLY, WE WANT A UNIVERSITY THAT IS. . .

1. Open for all, free for all, funded completely by the state but with autonomous democratic governance by faculty, staff, and students.
2. Opposed to the inequities generated and reinforced by racial capitalism (i.e., in terms of access to the university itself or in terms of access to participation)
3. Free of cost and inequalities, with freedom of thought freeing time to engage in texts (broadly defined) and to be curious, creative, and caring.

Practically, this means universities should support enough faculty to allow for smaller classes and room for relationships to develop while providing time for research and writing. Students should also have time to explore ideas, informally meet, and organize activities that intervene in the world as given. All university workers—including those who shape and maintain its physical space—should actively participate in the intellectual community. Finally, the university should be an open and welcoming place where the surrounding and extended community comes to share ideas and create knowledge.

WHAT IS ERODING HOPE FOR THE PUBLIC UNIVERSITY?

Our investigation led us into the murky waters of debt servicing fees, the covenants that require debts to be the first payment priority, and the cost of these fees for students whose own debt helps pay the institutional debt. We also examined the relationship between credit ratings and union organizing (an allegedly inverse relationship, according to Moody's). Finally, we gained a new appreciation for why so many financiers were sitting as trustees on higher education boards and the implications for democratic governance. We found that the logic of debt often determines the purpose and practice of higher education. It shapes program decisions, hiring practices, and was a significant part of a broader shift toward valuing education as a simple exchange of cash and "return on investment." This logic is also evident in the mechanisms of student debt, wherein students incur debt to attain higher education and then spend their lives feeding profits to financiers through interest payments.

This is the wider logic of the current stage of capitalism, "neoliberalism." This iteration of capitalism eschews any notion of the commons or public good and, instead, reduces everything to commodities and market competition. Another salient feature of neoliberalism is the misunderstanding that value arises from finance. We often forget that the bankers to whom students and our institutions are indebted produce nothing—they merely loan capital made possible by workers. The neoliberal political economy has social implications—it narrows how we know ourselves, each other, and our work; it creates an individualistic "common sense" driven by competition and measured only in monetary gains. In higher education, the debt economy has delivered adjuncts as gig workers, students tethered by debt well after graduation and throughout their lives, the erosion of a broad-based education, the elimination of programs that do not have a high return on investment (arts, history, literature, ethnic studies), and increasingly smaller spheres for creativity, critical analysis, and education as freedom. We must take on debt in order to first preserve public higher education, and then transform it into a space for liberation and racial and economic justice.

This common sense has us measuring the effectiveness of college by graduates' income levels (i.e., their return on investment). Such a measure obscures the range of reasons someone might want a four-year degree and ignores the social stratification and income inequality already baked into college opportunities and experiences. This common sense is shaped by the austerity, individualism, and competition of the neoliberal moment. The commons (publicly shared spaces serving the public good) have been privatized and we must all individually either avoid or be entrapped by debt and despair. If we accept degrees of austerity (even as the rich grow richer), individualism (even as the pandemic and climate crisis reveal our intimate interconnections), and competition (despite the power of collective action), then we will remain bound to processes and decisions that allow financiers to overwhelm and undercut the democratic and liberatory potential of higher education.

This book exposes the common sense that makes the social construction of debt—shaped by the political economy and its cultural and social relations—seem natural. It normalizes the expectation that individuals will incur debt to meet basic needs like housing, healthcare, and education (now all private goods and individual struggles). Debt is the path to some modicum of security, even as it chains us to the demands of bankers and financiers, leaving us more insecure and tied to jobs that increasingly impose on our time and wellbeing. Capital distorts our sense of our world and ourselves; the debtor carries the moral burden of repaying the debt, while the ruling class walks free of obligation. The moral imperative is to pay your debt and to be ashamed if you do not (unless you are a billion-dollar bank, in which case, the government will bail you out). Personal shame lurks in conversations about debt, in language like debt *forgiveness*, not debt *cancellation*. Our struggles are said to be of our own making, not manifestations of the exploitation and ravages of capital. Despite its personal, concrete implications for most of our lives, debt is shrouded in mystery—a complicated and unknowable device only for the experts to understand.

INSTITUTIONAL DEBT IS A UNION ISSUE

We did not merely want to describe the problem of higher education debt. We wanted to organize to end it and open a space for the university we envisioned. It was significant that our discussions originated in the PHEW space. The knowledge of ourselves as workers underpinned our understanding of who needed to undo the web of finance capital entangling and distorting public higher education. It would be the workers, the union members, because we had the power. Control over and the promise for public higher education is a worker issue, a union issue, an issue for all of us looking to build public spaces and collective possibilities for our world.

Public education workers hold a critical position in the fight for justice and the commons. Certainly, under capitalism, education workers are tasked with reproducing the workers needed to maintain the system; however, education (particularly public education) is also a site of possibility. Public colleges and universities hold the barricade, protecting the idea of the commons—of shared public spaces accessible to all that meet public needs and are managed by the public. Demanding for a public university as the commons goes beyond defending jobs and accessibility. It insists that the "public" part of the *public university* remains central to its vision and practice. Importantly, the possibility of reshaping our social relations is latent in the public university to the degree that classrooms are sites of liberatory practice. Educators in PreK–12 public schools have shown us that education workers are well-positioned to fight for liberatory teaching and learning. Unionized education workers have long protected the commons of public education (e.g., fights for educator autonomy, ending high-stakes testing, opposing charter schools, and getting cops out of schools).

For narrow-minded "business unionists," the union's purview starts and stops at wages and benefits for specific workers. The fight to protect the 'public' in public universities is simply beyond the scope of these bread-and-butter demands. As Joe Burns' book *Class Struggle Unionism* (2022) shows, business unions are inclined to work with management, accept the terms of capital, and negotiate within those terms. Other kinds of unions also accept the structures and constraints of capitalism, despite their confrontational tactics. These so-called labor liberals seek to expand workers' piece of the pie without fully challenging the common sense that rules our culture and political economy (e.g., bosses, management, debt, the commodification of our very being).

For unions to fight for the public university as a site of potential liberation, they must be grounded in an emancipatory political project. They need a political vision. Furthermore, while our organizing starts in the workplace, its horizon is the restructuring of economic and social relations. This kind of union politics must confront management and, since Wall Street calls the shots on our campuses (e.g., through trustee seats, manipulation of credit ratings, and agreements that prioritize debt service fees above all else), financiers become the management to confront. This kind of union practice reaches beyond the union hall, into classrooms, and onto the streets to build the collective power to claim our political vision.

Our first challenge is to draw back the curtain, exposing financial machinations and their negative impacts on the university. Then, armed with a vision of what is right, we must organize to build the power to win that vision and defend the public good. Organized workers in public universities struggle for a profoundly democratic space of teaching and learning—the protecting and extending of the commons. Like our PreK–12 counterparts, university workers acting collectively can leverage the power of withholding our labor in the interest of the common good.

As we will explain in this book, institutional debt warps the public university from the inside. It reshapes goals and values, undermines democracy, and makes the university into yet another object from which to extract profit in the form of debt servicing fees. As class struggle unionists, we fight for working-class universities that prefigure the world we are building. Unions must understand and combat all that undermines the university as a democratic and liberatory space and articulate a clear vision for the university that serves our values and hopes. Unions should also more clearly identify the forces against which we are struggling, including capitalism and its effects on our economy and worldviews.

WHAT YOU WILL FIND HERE

This book both exposes how debt has come to threaten public universities and offers specific steps toward resistance and possibility. The chapters trace the debt economy, the particulars of debt financing in universities, and how we have organized. We also invite readers to begin organizing to cancel debt and win the universities we need. Systems of debt are complex, often intimidating, and induce shame. Those holding the strings of power are distant from the everyday lives of workers in universities. Furthermore, because debt undergirds our economy, targeting it implies dismantling the whole destructive system, which can leave us overwhelmed and demoralized. How do we educate others and ourselves about these systems? How do we unshroud the mystery and remove the shame of debt? What are our demands? How do we build enough power to claim the university for the people? The following pages outline how we met these challenges.

Chapter 1 provides a broad overview of the debt economy, how it has developed, and its function in the current neoliberal stage of capitalism. We examine the challenge of cutting the strings of debt and explore higher education's contradictory role (i.e., it reproduces the debt economy while also prefiguring new economic and social relations). In Chapter

2, we consider how debt financing operates in higher education institutions. Who are the players? How are decisions made, by whom, and where? We trace how higher education became trapped in debt and the implications for who is taught and what is taught. In particular, debt financing reinforces racism and inequality, not only by limiting access for poor students and students of color, but also by burdening certain institutions such that they cannot offer the same range of educational experiences as whiter, wealthier institutions. This chapter unravels the narrative of "budget shortfalls" and "overspending" to reveal how finance dictates campus budgets, resources, and even responses to collective action. After uncovering these forces and mechanisms undermining higher education, we turn to the question of organizing against campus debt and the particular challenges that need to be understood and overcome. Chapter 3 examines the challenges organizers face and, through examples, offers tips that might aid organizers in their work.

The last three chapters show what is possible when we organize. Chapter 4 takes us into the earliest stages of organizing on two public higher education campuses. We outline a model of political education that helps workers analyze campus debt, build their knowledge, and plant the seeds of collective action. Chapter 5 draws on organizing in the Massachusetts State Universities to show what can happen when initial organizing activities are scaled up to include multiple universities and a collective (and union-supported) push to name and fight debt financing. In Chapter 6, we scale up again to examine how debt financing, a hypercharged aspect of the madness of capitalism, has eroded every aspect of life in Puerto Rico—from the university to the electrical grid. In response, a movement of all workers is now naming debt as wrong and acting collectively to refuse the terms imposed by it.

Our vision contains our politics—economic and racial justice, the claiming of a commons, and education as liberation. This politics connects our struggles and sustains us. It refutes the world as currently constructed and denaturalizes capital, debt, and individualism. This politics only works for the horizon if it is grounded in the steps taken by organizing. This is why we share examples of workers investigating debt and its impact on their own universities. You will read about workers and students teaching each other to spread the news about campus debt. This organizing prefigures the world we are moving toward—workers managing their own affairs, acting collectively, naming the world they want, and creating it. The new world does not emerge after the old world is dismantled. The new world is here—right now—in our collective, deeply democratic, worker-led struggle.

CHAPTER ONE
THE UNIVERSITY IN A DEBT
ECONOMY

This chapter examines how debt structures the economy and how the economy structures universities. It identifies the pressure points and contradictions within this economic system that may indicate sites for intervention.

Debt dictates much of what does and does not happen in our universities. Debt-driven austerity determines the working conditions for faculty and staff, the educational experience for students, and, often, the affordable housing and employment opportunities for communities surrounding a campus. We approach debt as an invisible but powerfully efficient tool of governance that delimits what a university is and can be. Both because of and despite this, we position universities as sites of debt resistance. They are privileged arenas of struggle, places to build opposition to the debt economy writ large.

As Marx and Engels wrote over a century ago, capitalism digs its own grave. Neoliberal capitalists have planted the seeds of their own destruction by using debt to shape and control educational institutions. They erred when they decided to put debtors—faculty, staff, students, and universities themselves—in the same location. Historically, debtors have been hard to mobilize—we were burdened with never-ending work, separated by shame and guilt, and rarely had a common workplace. However, the contemporary university differs from the rest of the debt landscape. No other place in American society is literally flush with thousands of debtors gathered in the same place at the same time. Alone, this reality guarantees nothing, but it opens a potent possibility. Here, debtors can learn to organize together, liberate higher education from debt's pernicious bonds, and even envision a world beyond debt.

UNIVERSITIES: BOTH RESISTANT TO THE DEBT ECONOMY AND DETERMINED BY IT?

Universities play a special role in the debt economy. Although they reproduce it, they are also sites to develop radical thought, prefigure new forms of relating to others and the world, and question political economic systems. Try as they might, dominant political and economic forces cannot control all aspects of higher education all the time. Even in the most repressive situations, education always produces an excess: thoughts that cannot be delimited, experiences that escape surveillance and discipline. Struggles for autonomous education institutions that enable faculty, students, and staff to define and pursue their own interests—in which education itself is seen as a practice of autonomy—are fundamental to our vision.

This is not a hypothetical or aspirational vision of universities. Even under bleak conditions, universities and colleges persist as sites of radical thought; the vicious, reactionary battles over their funding, administration, and curriculum prove as much. As Ralph Wilson and Isaac Kamola note in their analysis of the Koch brothers' extensive creep into higher education, the "plutocratic libertarian class sees university campuses as critical to their strategy for social change and as a pipeline of ideas and talent."[1] One wonders if conservative reactionaries like the Koch brothers possess a stronger analysis of education's crucial political economic role than many progressive proponents of higher education. The conservative obsession with higher education is only surprising if one understands universities as somehow hovering slightly beyond society—floating just above everyday life.

Of course, universities and the social relations that govern them are firmly embedded within society. As the Brazilian philosopher Marilena Chaui reminds us, universities and society are not separate entities; no university operates with complete autonomy from the norms, governance, or economic realities of its society. In Chaui's words, a university "is not a separate reality but a historically determined expression of a determined society."[2] Put slightly dif-

[1] Ralph Wilson and Isaac Kamola, *Free Speech: Manufacturing a Campus Culture War* (London: Pluto Press, 2021), 3.

[2] Marilena Chauí, *Escritos Sobre a Universidade* (São Paulo: Editora UNESP, 2000), 34–35.

ferently, universities are inherently heteronomous, subject to external standards or norms. At best, they contain pockets of autonomous elements. Today's universities are shaped by the heteronomous force of financial capitalism (amongst others), specifically by credit and debt.

Despite this, many social justice movements consistently treat education policy, pedagogy, and educational institutions as sovereign provinces. They tacitly assume that education matters are somehow bracketed from the world beyond the school walls or campus greens. Struggles are often waged as individual campuses or, in the best case, across statewide systems. They rarely concern themselves with analyzing and intervening in the broader political economy. To be sure, victories for better teaching and learning conditions at places like Rutgers University[3] and the University of California system[4] are vital and need to be celebrated. Yet, these victories do not necessarily disrupt the debt economy. For example, Rutgers University's Board of Trustees raised tuition in response to the faculty union's historic victory to increase salaries and improve benefits and working conditions for faculty, graduate students, and

---

[3] Bryan Sacks and Michael Reagan, "Rutgers Strike Wins Big but More is Needed to Change Higher Education," *Labor Notes*, March 11, 2023, https://labornotes.org.

[4] Hannah Appel, "Tenant, Debtor, Worker, Student," *New York Review of Books*, February 8, 2023, https://www.nybooks.com.

staff.[5] According to the board's logic, the money to meet the union's new contract demands and the university's existing debt obligations had to come from *somewhere*. Rather than pull from the reserves—which might harm the university's credit rating—the board burdened students with further costs and debt. For the board, this solved two problems at once: increasing tuition generated more income for the university while also eroding the union's collective power by driving a wedge between faculty, students, and the tax-paying public.

The historical record is replete with examples of how social justice progress in higher education has been nullified and hollowed out by the debt economy. In the latter half of the twentieth century, faculty, students, and community activists in New York City won and sustained a brief period of free tuition and open admissions policies.[6] However, CUNY was forced to impose tuition and end its open admissions policy to pay its bills to creditors during the city's fiscal debt crisis in the seventies.[7] These examples illustrate how education realities are shaped by political economic factors. Without this kind of analysis, we fear that education move-

---

[5] Matt Trapani and Alex Zdan, "NJ taxpayers to pay millions in state aid Rutgers amid tuition increase," *New Jersey News 12*, July 12, 2023, https://newjersey.news12.com.

[6] Conor Tomás Reed, *New York Liberation School: Study and Movement for the People's University* (New York: Common Notions Press, 2023).

[7] Kim Phillips-Fein, *Fear City: New York's Fiscal Crisis and the Rise of Austerity Politics* (New York: Metropolitan Books, 2017).

ments may unwittingly limit their horizons and make strategic errors. We must change the economic system in which universities and colleges reside if we are to create a more equitable higher education system capable of addressing the root causes of inequality.

Understanding contemporary university realities demands a basic understanding of the neoliberal debt economy. We need not become experts in contemporary financial capitalism or master the jargon associated with debt and credit. We just need to understand how debt operates as an axis of power and influences political-economic-pedagogical economies. With this knowledge, we can build a movement that flips dominant asymmetrical creditor-debtor paradigms. We need to shed light on institutional debt as a tool of shadow governance in higher education. Importantly, it is organized debtors, not creditors, who hold the power to create an alternative university system.

THE NEOLIBERAL ECONOMY AS A DEBT ECONOMY

In a debt economy, public goods and services—from healthcare to higher education, housing to transportation systems—are financed through debt instead of tax-funded revenue. As Jackie Wang states, "Beginning in the 1970s, there was a revolt in the capitalist class that undermined the tax state and led to the transformation of public finance. Over the subsequent decades, the tax state was gradually transformed into the debt state"[8] as decreases in available tax revenue made individuals and public institutions in the United States and elsewhere more reliant on private debt to meet basic needs. Most of the world's nation-states have moved, according to Wolfgang Streeck, from "tax states to debt states," albeit at different rates and with differing degrees of intensity. Similarly, universities increasingly depend on student and private debt over public funding (i.e., from taxing wealth accumulation).

Neoliberal ideology, from the seventies onward, has reframed taxation. Taxes levied from income and property assets were no longer understood as contributions to a public good, but violations of individual freedom and toxic overreach from a meddling government. Tax revolts waged by individuals and corporations led to significant reductions in tax revenue around the world.[9] The oft-repeated neoliberal austerity narrative convinced policymakers and the general public alike to drastically cut local and federal spending on public goods. This combination of decreasing tax revenue and draconian austerity measures has radically altered private and

---

[8] Jackie Wang, *Carceral Capitalism* (Cambridge, MA: The MIT Press, 2018), 14.

[9] Wolfgang Streeck, *Buying Time: The Delayed Crisis of Democratic Capitalism* (Brooklyn: Verso, 2017); Isaac William Martin, *The Permanent Tax Revolt: How the Property Tax Transformed American Politics* (Palo Alto: Stanford University Press, 2008); Melinda Cooper, *Family Values: Between Neoliberalism and the New Social Conservatism* (New York: Zone Books, 2017), 215–258.

public life. To make up for the lack of public funding, free or low-cost services were curtailed while access to credit was democratized. The expansion of credit markets and subsequent reliance on debt financing for mere survival has enormous implications for governments, public institutions, and individuals.

A state run on debt faces intense costs. As Streeck explains, states accumulate mountains of debt that they must finance with an ever-greater share of their revenues.[10] States do not run deficits because of outlandish spending on public goods (the austerity narrative promoted by the creditor class). Rather, they face a revenue problem resulting from years of lowering taxes on the wealthy.[11] In Streeck's words, "Not *high spending*, but *low receipts*, are the cause of government debt."[12] His book, *Buying Time: The Delayed Crisis of Democratic Capitalism*, argues that neoliberal-era governments' limits on taxation have hindered their ability to meet the demands of the post-WWII welfare state.

As tax states became debt states, wealth and power have accumulated in the hands of financial capitalists, with serious implications for the notions of democracy and sovereignty. The former chair of the United States Federal Reserve, Alan Greenspan, once matter-of-factly declared, with-

---

[10] Streeck, *Buying Time,* 72–73.

[11] Streeck, *Buying Time*, 76.

[12] Streeck, *Buying Time*, 66, italics in original.

out a ripple of protest, that: "We are fortunate that, thanks to globalization, policy decisions in the US have been largely replaced by global market forces. . . . National security aside, it hardly matters any difference who will be the next president. *The world is governed by market forces*."[13] This remarkable claim gives credence to the fact that we live under the power of what Andrew Ross adroitly calls the "creditocracy."[14] Governance in the interests of the creditor class (re)produces a society where access to essentials like education will always be financed through debt.

Now, more than ever, it is necessary to understand the economy as politics and economic forces as political forces.[15] Inversely, we "can't understand politics without relating them to markets."[16] Debt crises—like those many universities, cities, and countries now face—are the result of political (not strictly economic) decisions that benefit the creditor class. Such political decisions are radically undemocratic. Financial capitalists wield monetary debt as a political weapon; they hold state budgets and currencies hostage and demand austerity reforms before granting credit. Many nation-states and their public institutions are increasingly

---

[13] Alan Greenspan, quoted in Streeck, *Buying Time*, 85, emphasis added.

[14] Andrew Ross, *Creditocracy: And the Case for Debt Refusal* (New York: OR Books, 2013).

[15] Streeck, *Buying Time*, xv.

[16] Streeck, *Buying Time*, lxiii.

beholden to private financiers that demand advanced debt payment pledges in the form of tax revenue. The states lose power, while creditors (not elected officials or the people) become the regulators of society.[17]

THE LONG HISTORY OF DEBT IN HIGHER EDUCATION

Indebtedness is not a new phenomenon for universities. Some of the nation's first private and public colleges relied on loans from private patrons. The slave trade also played a major role in financing early American higher education, with enslaved people sometimes used to settle university debts for payment in lieu of tuition.[18] One contemporary group of radical thinkers, the Abolitionist University Studies Collective, has shown how universities have used debt to extract wealth from people and communities.[19] Universities in Puerto Rico are also familiar with debt as a tool of colonial extraction in education. There is nothing "new" about universities' contemporary dependency on debt; however,

---

[17] Étienne Balibar, "Politics of Debt," *Postmodern Culture* 23, no. 3 (2013): 1–35.

[18] Craig Steven Wilder, *Ebony and Ivy: Race, Slavery, and the Troubled History of America's Universities* (New York: Bloomsbury Press, 2013).

[19] Abigail Boggs, Eli Meyerhoff, Nick Mitchell, and Zach Schwartz-Weinstein, "Abolitionist University Studies: An Invitation," *Abolition Journal*, August 28, 2019, https://abolitionjournal.org.

the intensity of debt reliance reached historic levels under neoliberalism.

In the wake of the Great Depression, the New Deal offered a radical vision for social welfare programs that enfranchised labor unions and secured workers' rights to stabilize the economy. However, by the sixties, education had supplanted labor as the mainstay of the social welfare state. Lydon B. Johnson's Great Society program emphasized tax cuts and education. The federal government rejected direct economic interventions (e.g., income redistribution, public employment, or labor union rights) in favor of programs to "equip the poor with the tools they needed 'to earn the American standard of living by their own efforts and contributions.'"[20] This era also saw the start of individualist, even consumerist, federal support for public higher education, which comes from tuition subsidies for students, not direct funding for universities.

This had particularly acute consequences given the United States' employer-based welfare state. Unlike many other industrialized nations, health insurance, paid sick leave, living wages, and pensions are provided by employers (when they are provided at all). The jobs that provide these basic welfare provisions increasingly require col-

[20] Harvey Kantor, "From the New Deal to the Great Society," *Educational Researcher* 24, no. 3 (1995): 4–11; Harvey Kantor and Robert Lowe, "Class, Race and the Emergency of Federal Education Policy: From the New Deal to the Great Society," *Educational Researcher* 24, no. 3 (1995): 4–11.

lege degrees, meaning the political and economic pressures on higher education have intensified well beyond academic merits. A college degree represents far more than a diploma; for many, it provides the best shot at securing retirement or health insurance.

INVENTING TUITION SUBSIDIES: FROM THE GI BILL TO THE HIGHER EDUCATION ACT

In 1940, only a slim minority of young Americans (less than 10 percent) attended college.[21] The GI Bill, which rewarded surviving soldiers with free higher education, changed that. It was the nation's first federal education policy to mass enroll people in colleges. This, and cheap mortgages for white veterans, helped the government absorb sixteen million returning soldiers. The Bill channeled mostly white men into college degrees, which led to middle-class occupations that could service veterans' mortgages and provide a breadwinner's wage.

Subsidizing higher education also kept disaffected veterans from jumping directly into a labor movement bursting with militancy. A 1947 Bureau of Labor Statistics report noted that the six months following World War II "marked the most concentrated period of labor-management strife" to

---

[21] Claudia Goldin and Lawrence F. Katz, "The Shaping of Higher Education: The Formative Years in the United States, 1890 to 1940," *Journal of Economic Perspectives* 13, no. 1 (1999): 37–62.

date.[22] Workers no longer tolerated the restrained wages justified by the war, especially since the end of wartime price controls meant that living costs spiked while wages flattened. In 1946, some 4.6 million workers—newly unbridled from no-strike pledges—went on strike for weeks at a time, with the average strike lasting twenty-four days. Rather than backing workers' demands for greater wage protections, the federal government passed the 1947 Taft-Hartley Act, which limited workers' organizing power and protected management's ability to thwart unions. Meanwhile, the GI Bill subsidized white veterans' tuition, charting their path to higher wages and keeping them safely away from erupting shop floors.

The GI Bill was also the first major plank in the tuition subsidy model. The federal government paid up to $4,400 (more than $51,000 in 2022 dollars) for each soldier's degree and living expenses.[23] This tuition reimbursement system provided financial assistance for *students,* not funding directly to higher education. However, it was still effective at opening the university's doors, even if the federal government supported education one student at a time (in 1949, 70 percent of male college graduates were veterans).

---

[22] United States Department of Labor, Bureau of Labor Statistics, *Work Stoppages Caused by Labor-Management Disputes in 1946.*

[23] Keith W. Olson, "The G. I. Bill and Higher Education: Success and Surprise," *American Quarterly* 25, no. 5 (1973): 596–610; Paul H. Berkhart, ed., *No Child Left Behind: Issues and Developments* (New York: Nova Science Publishers, 2008), 63.

Over the next decade, as the Cold War loomed, the federal government once again stepped up its higher education investments to assist the war effort. Rather than merely sop up the aftermath of war, the university would build a labor force specifically designed for wars to come. In 1958, one year after the Soviet Union launched Sputnik 1, President Dwight D. Eisenhower signed the National Defense Education Act (NDEA), which comprehensively funded science and technology education. The NDEA was motivated by an over-whelming fear that America's science classrooms were somehow inferior to those in the USSR. The Act also established the first federal student loan program, which provided direct low-interest loans for students enrolled in defense-related fields (e.g., science, mathematics, and foreign languages). This continued the trend of investing in tuition subsidies and narrowed the target to specific fields of study.[24]

In the early sixties, economists noticed that countries with higher educational attainment also had more robust economic growth. Thus, a new policy paradigm began to emerge. Mainstream politicians—heavily influenced by the economist Theodore Schultz—embraced the idea that educa-tion could transform humans into a resource much like capital. Schultz believed cultivating human capital via education would ameliorate a harden-

---

[24] Melinda Cooper, *In Loco Parentis: Human Capital, Student Debt, and the Logic of Family Investment. Family Values. Between Neoliberal-ism and the New Social Conservatism* (New York: Zone Books, 2017).

ing system of economic inequality: "Truly, the most distinctive feature of our economic system is the growth in human capital. . . . Without it there would be only hard manual work and poverty except for those who have income from property."[25] Education offered an almost magical way to improve the national economy, bolster national security, and provide upward mobility for the poor. All this without the need to overhaul the capitalist system!

Key liberal policymakers were attracted to Schultz's human capital model and the framing of higher education as a profitable investment. One such devotee was Clark Kerr, a labor economist and president of the University of California system from 1958 to 1967. Kerr set to work ensuring the university would become the key vehicle for building national economic power, akin to "what the railroads did for the second half of the last century and the automobile for the first half of this century."[26] He was especially keen to include women, people of color, and low-income students. This program for higher education powerfully consolidated several key prongs of the liberal accord—it would prepare the "knowledge workers" necessary for the country's petrochemical, agrochemical, and defense industries while also committing to domes-

---

[25] Theodore W. Schultz, "Investment in Human Capital," *American Economic Association* 51, no. 5 (1961): 1035–39.

[26] Clark Kerr, *The Uses of the University* (Cambridge: Harvard University Press, 1963), 66.

tic social inclusion. In 1965, this vision of higher education became law with President Lyndon B. Johnson's Higher Education Act (HEA).

The HEA created the basic architecture for today's student loan industry. Under the HEA, student loans originated with private banks but were backed by the federal government. At first, these loans were only available to low-income borrowers, but eventually, all students became eligible. This significant expansion of the student loan business proved quite profitable for private banks, as they took all the profits and absorbed none of the risks. Importantly, the HEA also distributed federal aid to historically Black colleges and universities, opened bridge programs encouraging first-generation students to pursue college degrees, and paved the way for the Pell Grant program, which allocates federal funds to low-income college students. Though hardly perfect, this federal funding system enabled an unprecedented number of students to enroll in higher education at no (or very low) cost. Nevertheless, the HEA continued to provide individualized access to increasingly costly higher education instead of creating free public higher education for all.

By the mid-sixties, the nation had been plunged into a deeply unpopular war in Vietnam and racist and sexist legacies had unleashed new currents at home. Universities provided a critical gathering point for social activists and social movement organizing around Black Power, women's liberation, free speech, and antiwar. Students were not content to simply learn about the structures of the world; they fought to transform them. Many of these movements pushed back against the "knowledge society" and its militaristic and capitalist endpoints for education. If education was the means to build a new society, it could also dismantle a dysfunctional one. However, this liberatory capacity quickly pushed policymakers and pundits to oppose free and subsidized higher education.

HIGHER EDUCATION AS PRIVATE PROPERTY

The unwittingly radical potential of public higher education proved dangerous as it could be harnessed into social movements capable of challenging the status quo. The elites wanted education to fulfill the promise of human capital but only when chained to its economic role and divorced from radical possibilities. After witnessing "intolerant radicals" protest at the University of Chicago in 1969, the economist Milton Friedman argued that "We must do some drastic rethinking if we are to preserve the university as the home of reason, persuasion, and free discussion."[27] For Friedman, this meant shifting the costs of education onto students. He considered education to be a kind of capital—basically, private property; its cost should be shouldered by the individual beneficiary, not the public. He adamantly opposed state investment

[27] Milton Friedman, *An Economist's Protest: Columns on Political Economy* (Glen Ridge, NJ: Thomas Horton & Daughters, 1972), 191–92.

in collective education, instead favoring a voucher style system for individuals (much like how the GI Bill provided grants to individual veterans rather than eliminating tuition). Friedman's design for higher education undergirded the 1958 Treasury-funded student loans. However, Friedman sought a long-lasting policy framework to actualize his ideology. He found its executor in Ronald Reagan.

Almost immediately after becoming governor of California, Reagan campaigned to impose tuition and fees on the state's previously free university system as a thinly veiled punishment for student activism. Guided by Friedman's free market wisdom, Reagan recast free tuition—hitherto a beloved public benefit—as an unfair public entitlement that forced taxpayers to fund the reading habits of communists, gays, and bra-burning peaceniks. Once elected president, Reagan doubled down on the widely held beliefs that college should be funded through tuition and tuition financed through loans. While Democratic and Republican legislators disagreed on the mechanics of the student loan market, both parties agreed on its basic premise: the ticket to higher education would be bought through borrowed money, not state funding.

This logic pushed the costs of higher education onto students and turned universities into debtors. In the seventies and eighties, states cut public colleges' and universities' budgets in exchange for capital gains tax cuts. This enabled private equity and hedge fund managers to amass billions of dollars while choking public institutions of necessary funding. As sociologist Charlie Eaton documents, elite universities themselves regularly participated in this scheme, often through clever tax avoidance strategies. The 2017 Paradise Papers leak confirmed that many top universities have established offshore shell companies to dodge taxes on their endowment funds' investment activities.[28]

In the first few years of the 2000s, university administrators began to make up for cuts in public funding by taking on more institutional debt. This happened quietly in boardrooms and finance offices. In the first twenty years of the twenty-first century, the amount of long-term debt held by public institutions tripled on a per student basis (see Figure 1 below).[29] The total amount of long-term debt held by public institutions increased 482 percent[30] between 1989 (about $30 billion) and 2021(nearly $175 billion).[31] As schools borrow

---

[28] Charlie Eaton, *Bankers in the Ivory Tower the Troubling Rise of Financiers in US Higher Education* (Chicago: The University of Chicago Press, 2022), 52–54.

[29] A better point of comparison here would be the amount of principal, interest, and fees paid each year on institutional debt. This is not included in any centralized data that the authors are aware of and would have to be culled from individual institutions' annual financial statements. Therefore, overall growth of long-term debt from IPEDS data was used instead.

[30] Monetary values compared over time have been adjusted for inflation as of November 2022, when much of the data was originally pulled. "Snapshot-in-time" monetary values have not been adjusted.

[31] The variables of "Long-term debt," "Balance owed on principal at end of year," and "Debt related to Property Plant and Equipment"

more, greater proportions of their budgets are set aside to service debt interest and fee payments. Between 2003 and 2012, university annual interest payments jumped from $6 billion to $11 billion. Similarly, in 2003, public colleges spent an average of $519 on interest payments per full-time student each year; by 2012, they were spending $750 on interest payments per student—a nearly 45 percent increase.[32] Universities and colleges currently face

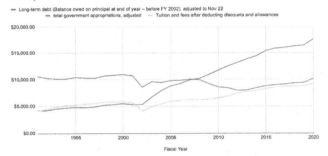

Long-term debt, government (federal, state, and local) appropriations, tuition & fees: amount in USD$, adjusted to Nov 22, per FTE (full-time equivalent) student, public 2- and 4-year+ institutions, from IPEDS self-reported data

— Long-term debt (Balance owed on principal at end of year – before FY 2002), adjusted to Nov 22
— total government appropriations, adjusted   — Tuition and fees after deducting discounts and allowances

This graph displays data for public institutions (data reporting for private institutions only began in 2010). The rate of increase of debt was similar for private institutions, although the amount of debt per student was nearly three times higher at private colleges and universities.

---

were retrieved from the US Department of Education, National Center for Education Statistics, Integrated Postsecondary Education Data System (IPEDS), 1989–2021 on March 15, 2023. These variables are used throughout. There was an IPEDS field reporting change (from "balance owed on principal at end of year" to "long-term debt") for public institutions in 2002. This analysis uses both measures.

[32] Charlie Eaton, Jacob Habinek, Adam Goldstein, Cyrus Dioun, Daniela Garda Santibanez Godoy, and Robert Osley-Thomas, "The

the lowest levels of state funding in decades despite student and university debt being at all-time highs. Colleges and universities use student debt to leverage institutional debt; they pledge future student tuition as a revenue source to make payments on institutional debt.[33] In the last two years, the problem of student debt has garnered significant public attention, and relief is understood to be politically and economically necessary. However, the problem of institutional debt—and its connection to student debt—has largely evaded the spotlight.

As institutional debt rises, university budgets must increasingly prioritize debt servicing over students. The university's debt repayment is its first order of business—before educating students, employing workers, or stewarding knowledge. Administrators freeze faculty salaries, promote adjunct contracts and weaken their protections, shutter "unprofitable" humanities programs, and pack classrooms like sardine cans to satiate creditors. Clearly, these chilling dynamics have devastating consequences for education.

CONCLUSION

Contemporary social justice movements negotiate difficult terrain when fighting against the entire structure of a global economic order. Movements

---

Financialization of US Higher Education," *Socio-Economic Review* 14, no. 3 (2016): 507–35.

[33] Bob Meister, "They Pledged Your Tuition," *University Council-AFT*, n.d., https://ucaft.org.

must seek victories in both their immediate and long-term struggles. Many activists want to target the individuals responsible for making "bad" decisions—the politicians or corporate elite who work to maintain smooth political and economic conditions for themselves while leaving the rest behind. Such movements target evil henchmen and fight for economic concessions that ameliorate the precarity of twenty-first-century capitalism. Fights for better wages and increased benefits (e.g., sick or childcare days) aim to make life just a bit more bearable in the current system.

These reform efforts matter—a lot. But they are just that, reform movements that temporarily alleviate suffering under capitalism. We must constantly ask whether and how these reforms threaten capitalist social relations and modes of production that (re)produce gross inequities, racial and gender hierarchies, and neocolonial rule. Following Rosa Luxemburg, we might aspire for our campaigns to serve revolutionary goals, not merely reformist ones. What's the difference? Reform-based campaigns treat reforms as ends in themselves: we can pack up and go home after winning the wage increase, a few more sick days, a more culturally diverse table or once we have fired a boss, administrator, or morally bankrupt politician. Nevertheless, the system that produces and reproduces societal ills remains intact, stultifying revolutionary potential. In contrast, revolution addresses and changes the root causes of oppression. It aims to replace one system of rule with another, end one type of political economy to construct an alternative.

The authors of this book ultimately take a nuanced both/and approach to analysis and organizing in the contemporary debt economy. We seek to *both* develop theoretical insights to aid tactical planning for reform *and* create analysis that contributes to long-term strategic objectives for radically transforming the dominant system. We hope to support, uplift, and highlight debt abolition campaigns that target individual careerists and accomplices of evil doing and the struggles for basic economic and cultural rights that guarantee the dignity of all people. At the same time, we recognize that inclusion in the dominant system and fights to make life a little less difficult in the current order are necessary (but insufficient). If we abolish debts but leave the system producing debts active, then there is still work to do. Planning either reform or revolution in higher education—or better, planning reforms that hasten revolution—necessitates an analysis of the debt economy. Such an analysis may be rooted in universities but has the potential to extend beyond them into broader social struggles. To oversimplify our case, debt is at the heart of the neoliberal economy and should be centered in any theoretical, tactical, and strategic plan to transform our education institutions and the political economy they exist within. Far too often, education reformers misidentify the true culprits and subsequently misdirect efforts at change.

One lesson worth heeding comes from *The Grapes of Wrath*, one of the most moving American novels about life in debt. The novel chronicles the story of an indebted family of farmers, the Joads, who have been evicted from their land. They are victims of an insatiable ontologically indistinguishable "monster [that] has to have profits all the time." The tenants survive the Great Depression by nourishing bonds of solidarity with one another as they resist debt-imposed injustice. In one memorable scene, an old family acquaintance comes, atop a tractor, to clear the land and bulldoze a tenant's house. He's got orders to follow. The tenant quickly realizes that the driver is part of a machine, merely ancillary to something larger than himself. He desperately seeks someone real, or something concrete, to fight back against. If he shoots the driver, he will just be replaced. If he targets the bank president or board of directors, the tenant would still have to deal with the profit-hungry system the president and board serve. Perplexed and facing starvation, the tenant finally asks: "But where does it stop? Who can we shoot? I don't aim to starve to death before I kill the man that's starving me." The driver gets to the heart of the matter: "I don't know. Maybe there's nobody to shoot. Maybe the thing isn't man at all."

Like the dispossessed farmer, progressive circles often direct indignation at individuals: administrators, state government officials, trustees, and others who pull the strings of austerity. However, like the tractor driver, they serve a larger force. We can remove *a person* from the (tractor) chair, but the chair remains. Replacing one cast of characters running our universities with another more progressive one will not stop the machine they are accountable to. It will keep plowing ahead in directions that favor private creditors over the public good.

Our taxation and debt system creates rampant wealth inequalities that are reflected within higher education. The debt economy monster drains the lifeblood out of higher education and feeds the growth of social inequality. However, if we properly diagnose the root causes of higher education inequality and form bonds of debtor resistance, we can put it to rest. Higher education is one of many sites of struggle from which to challenge the debt economy. While we do not think that winning university debt abolition would overthrow the debt economy, we believe that it is a strategic institution from which to collectively wage a battle against financial capitalism. Within the financial capitalist debt economy, debtors will always be capable of building autonomous power to disrupt debt exploitation and extraction. In these pages, we acknowledge our potential to bolster the capacity of autonomous debt struggles, wherever they emerge.

CHAPTER TWO
UNIVERSITY DEBT FINANCING: THE CAST OF CHARACTERS

Public colleges and universities—like other public services without adequate funding—increasingly rely on debt to continue with basic functions. This transforms them into machines for private wealth extraction at the expense of students, workers, and communities. The pervasive reality of racial capitalism means that debt financing most brutally affects campuses serving students of color. Campus activists are used to fighting university management, trustees, and state officials that defund their public institutions. However, we are less familiar with the shadowy private entities that increasingly pull the strings of our familiar public adversaries. In the public sector, we tend to feel more removed from financialization despite public colleges and universities being fully immersed in the debt economy's manipulations. A major challenge for organizers is the relative invisibility of debt as a governing force. Indeed, we are frogs boiling in the pot of institutional debt and are just now becoming aware of it.

This chapter exposes the unfamiliar institutional players that extract public resources from higher education. Players like credit rating agencies and underwriters are not individual targets, but rather institutional actors that push and pull the levers of the debt economy. To reclaim our institutions for the public good and liberation, we must understand how they currently operate. An accurate analysis of debt should strive to overturn this oppressive system (with some reform steps along the way). Jockeying for a better position within the system (e.g., improving credit ratings or struggling for slightly less onerous rates and fees) is a waste of time if debt continues to siphon wealth, surveil, and control.

If you find this chapter trying, keep in mind that our financial overlords want you to feel like such issues are too complicated for regular folks to understand. They are not. The following pages examine some of the obvious and less obvious players. The university is the borrower taking on debt. The banks are creditors doing the lending and collecting interest. There are also intermediaries, including credit rating companies, underwriters, and insurers, who are enriched by the institutional debt system.

THE BORROWERS

The first institutional player is the borrower, who receives money and is obligated to repay it with interest and fees. In the case of higher education institutional debt, the borrower is the university. The decision to borrow is made by top administrators (chancellors or presidents) and members of the governing board (trustees or regents). They sign up for all the strings attached to debt through an antidemocratic and opaque process that never consults students, faculty, and staff. Students and workers are unlikely to even know about—let alone have access to—the meetings in which borrowing decisions are made. We must dig through purposely complex financial documents to confirm how much debt exists. Yet, the students and workers bear the brunt of campus debt (in addition to the student, medical, credit card, and other debts they have as individuals in a debt economy). Students' tuition and fees generate money to pay off debts, while workers must make do with fewer resources to save on costs, creating untenable working conditions.

Universities borrow for many reasons. Some borrow to build amenities that will hopefully attract wealthier and more lucrative out-of-state students that can make up for withdrawn state funding.[1] For example, the sprawling flagship University of Massachusetts Amherst campus (like many public universities) has used debt to build new luxury student residences,[2] renovate its highly-ranked dining

---

[1] In the United States, most public colleges and universities have different tuition rates for residents of the state and those who live outside of the state when they apply to college. Out-of-state students are charged higher rates. International students are often charged even more.

[2] After hitting limits on debt, UMass administration turned to public-private partnerships for dormitory construction—a pattern familiar to less resourced public colleges.

halls, and construct a new student union.[3] Lower-ranked schools tend to suffer deeper budget cuts. These schools, which serve most of the students of color in the United States, use debt to repair crumbling buildings and maintain the very basics of university space. UMass Boston—a commuter campus primarily serving working-class students of color—used debt to repair literally disintegrating classroom buildings and an unsafe underground parking garage. To offset payments on this construction debt, the board of trustees required the university to slash academic programs and lay off workers.[4] Nationally recognized, one-of-a-kind centers were put on the chopping block, including institutes for Black, Latinx, and Native American culture. The UMass Board of Trustees never consulted (or even informed) the Amherst or Boston campus communities or the wider public about these debt decisions. Students remained unaware that a growing percentage of their tuition bills went to servicing debt.[5]

The line between borrower and creditor is increasingly blurred as trustees and top university administrators keep close relationships with the financier class, the people and organizations that

[3] Yawu Miller, "UMass students carry schools' debt," *The Bay State Banner*, September 21, 2022, https://www.baystatebanner.com.

[4] The Coalition to Save UMB, "Crumbling Foundations: Privatization and UMass Boston's Financial Crisis," *FSU-UMass Boston*, August 2017, https://fsu.umb.edu.

[5] Joanna Gonsalves, Rich Levy, Gayathri Raja, Tyler Risteen, "Revealing Massachusetts Campus Debt," *Massachusetts Teacher Association*, n.d., https://massteacher.org.

extract profit from investing or lending money. They often move in the same elite social circles (e.g., private clubs and galas) and may have attended the same elite Ivy League schools. Many trustees are themselves financiers.[6] For instance, Governor Gray Davis appointed the private equity investor, billionaire Richard Blum, to the University of California Board of Regents. After his first twelve-year term, Blum was reappointed by Governor Edmund Brown.[7] During this long tenure, Blum worked hard to appoint his network of financiers to top positions in the university administration.[8] These social ties—between executive management of universities and those who control the funds—are seen as a career asset as higher education plunges deeper into debt financing.

However, top managers are also charged with upholding the missions of public institutions, which generally include affordability and accessibility. Borrowing private capital sits uncomfortably with such public missions. For instance, the chancellor of the University of Massachusetts upholds the university's mission to "provide an affordable and accessible education of high quality and to conduct programs of research and public ser-

---

[6] Charlie Eaton, *Bankers in the Ivory Tower the Troubling Rise of Financiers in US Higher Education* (Chicago: The University of Chicago Press, 2022).

[7] University of California, "Regent Emeritus Richard C. Blum," *University of California Board of Regents*, n.d., https://regents.universityofcalifornia.edu.

[8] Eaton, *Bankers in the Ivory Tower.*

vice that advance knowledge and improve the lives of the people of the Commonwealth, the nation, and the world."[9] Yet, the covenant binding the University of Massachusetts to its creditors says nothing about affordability. Its hundreds of pages require that tuition revenue be transferred to pay the debt in a timely and binding manner; debt repayment must be prioritized over all other spending. Therefore, the debt-governed university imposes cuts and layoffs on the very workforce that supplies the high-quality education promised in its mission statement.

Public universities take on debt due to a variety of different pressures, including the withdrawal of public funding. In the hyperdrive of colonial extraction in Puerto Rico, the public university was forced into the role of the borrower in an even more direct way. As we detail in Chapter 6, the University of Puerto Rico itself has a relatively low debt burden. However, the debt restructuring imposed on Puerto Rico has meant that the university must implement draconian cuts to repay the debt of the island as a whole.

THE CREDITORS

Many colleges, universities, and related government authorities issue bonds to raise (i.e., borrow) money. Such municipal bonds were tradition-

---

[9] University of Massachusetts Amherst, "Mission," *UMass Amherst*, n.d., https://www.umass.edu.

ally used by city and state governments to borrow money for public projects like repairing infrastructure and building new facilities. Bonds have normalized the shift from tax-financed public goods to debt-financed public goods, with the outstanding municipal bonds market totaling $4 trillion dollars in 2022.[10] These bonds have long-term fixed rates and are taken out for decades-long terms. This means that universities have pledged tuition and fees from students who are not yet born to repay the debt.

Municipal bonds are an attractive, low-risk asset for investors. This minimal risk is ensured by terms that guarantee a return to the creditor and prioritize debt repayment over keeping universities affordable or treating workers fairly.[11] Municipal bonds' interest payments are also not subjected to federal (and sometimes state and local) taxes.[12] Ironically, profits on municipal bonds generate no public revenue through taxation.

Banks, insurance companies, mutual funds, and individuals all invest in municipal bonds and receive biannual payments of interest and a portion of the principal amount loaned. According to the Federal Reserve, about 40 percent of municipal

---

[10] SIMFA, "US Municipal Bond Statistics," *SIMFA*, July 5, 2023, https://www.sifma.org.

[11] Alex Katsomitros, "The Emerging University Bonds Market," *World Finance*, n.d., https://www.worldfinance.com.

[12] Cooper Howard, "When to Consider Munis from Outside Your Home State," *Charles Schwab*, April 26, 2023, https://www.schwab.com.

bonds in 2022 were held by individual households (this number is down from 54 percent in 2004). However, the individual category is misleading: it includes many types of creditors like private equity funds, personal trusts, and hedge funds. Other creditors holding municipal bonds include financial funds (e.g., mutual funds, exchange-traded funds, closed-end funds, public employee retirement funds), banks, and insurance companies (e.g., life insurance, property insurance). A small but growing portion of municipal bonds are also owned by foreign entities.[13]

THE UNDERWRITERS

While the borrower-creditor relationship is relatively straightforward, several other actors contribute to the plunder of public higher education. Municipal bond underwriters are intermediary corporations that buy bonds from universities and then resell them to public investors with other debts they own.[14] They expect to buy the bonds at a lower price and then sell them to creditors for a profit. The average difference between the price bought and sold was 0.81 percent between 1988

---

[13] John Bagley, Marcelo Vieira, and Ted Hamlin, "Trends in Municipal Securities Ownership," Municipal Securities Rulemaking Board, June 2022, https://www.msrb.org.

[14] Casey Dougal, Pengjie Gao, William J. Mayew, and Christopher A. Parsons, "What's in a (School) Name? Racial Discrimination in Higher Education Bond Markets," *Journal of Financial Economics* 134, no. 3 (2019): 570–90.

and 2010.[15] The tepid attempts to regulate bank profiteering after the Great Recession did not affect municipal bond underwriters. Underwriting corporations like Bank of America and Merrill Lynch continue to prioritize their profits over protecting the interests of the taxpayers.

A 2019 study confirmed that historically Black colleges and universities (HBCUs) pay higher underwriting fees than non-HBCUs, even when other factors like credit rating are held constant. Once again, we see how inextricable the debt economy is from racial capitalism, marking Black people and institutions for intensified economic exploitation. Municipal bonds issued in US counties with more Black residents come with significantly higher fees.[16] Familiar banks (e.g., Citigroup and Barclays) also extract staggering underwriting fees from the Puerto Rican government—$1.6 billion between 2000 and 2016. With full public funding for our universities, there would be no need for underwriters or their fees.

THE CREDIT RATING AGENCIES

An oligarchy of immensely profitable credit rating companies (Moody's, Standard & Poor's (S&P Global), and to a lesser extent, Fitch) issue college and university credit ratings based on their sup-

---

[15] Dougal et al., "What's in a (School) Name."

[16] Alex Annan Abakah and Jiayan Li, "Is There a Racial Bias in Underwriter Fees? Evidence from U.S. County Government Bond Issuance," *Public Finance & Management* 21, no.1 (2022): 57–82.

posed likelihood of future loan defaults. The inputs for these ratings are subjective and only discussed behind closed doors, in private meetings between the credit rating agencies and the college finance officers.[17] As political scientist Timothy Sinclair put it, "Ratings provide a disciplinary force on institutions that can change what they do and how they operate. . . . This form of discipline is covert and unaccountable."[18] The credit rating agencies are the guard dogs of Wall Street bankers investing in public higher education. They guard the investment and enforce the bankers' agenda to extract profit from our public institutions.[19]

Credit ratings determine the costs of debt financing, with lower credit ratings generating more money for the creditors. Yet, credit rating agencies are actually quite bad at predicting defaults, as was dramatically demonstrated by the financial crisis of 2007–8. According to government regulators, Moody's and S&P Global made key contributions to the Great Recession[20] by issuing high credit rat-

[17] Giulia Mennillo, *Credit Rating Agencies* (New York: Columbia University Press, 2022), 41.

[18] Timothy J. Sinclair, *To the Brink of Destruction: America's Rating Agencies and Financial Crisis* (Ithaca: Cornell University Press, 2021).

[19] Eleni Schirmer, "It's Not Just Students Drowning in Debt. Colleges Are Too!" *The Nation*, November 20, 2020, https://www.thenation.com.

[20] The National Commission on the Causes of the Financial and Economic Crisis in the United States' *Financial Crisis Inquiry Report* concluded that "the failures of credit rating agencies were essential cogs in the wheel of financial destruction. The three credit rating agencies were key enablers of the financial meltdown. The

ings to risky financial instruments that eventually (inevitably) disintegrated and facilitated an economic collapse. Despite some reforms, there are still fundamental problems with how credit rating agencies operate. They remain incredibly powerful and profitable not because they provide accurate information about risk—the big players in finance generally ignore these ratings[21]—but because the rating has a significant impact on an institution's ability to access debt financing and at what cost.[22]

Counterintuitively, the debt issuers (i.e., soon-to-be borrowers) pay for this all-important rating assessment. Moody's charges between $1,500 and $2,400,000 in fees "based on a variety of factors, such as the type of rating being assigned, the com-

---

mortgage-related securities at the heart of the crisis could not have been marketed and sold without their seal of approval. Investors relied on them, often blindly. In some cases, they were obligated to use them, or regulatory capital standards were hinged on them. This crisis could not have happened without the rating agencies. Their ratings helped the market soar and their downgrades through 2007 and 2008 wreaked havoc across markets and firms."; United States Senate Permanent Subcommittee on Investigations, "Wall Street and the Financial Crisis: Anatomy of a Financial Collapse," Senate Committee on Homeland Security & Governmental Affairs, April 13, 2011, https://www.hsgac.senate.gov.

[21] Frank Partnoy, "How and Why Credit Rating Agencies Are Not Like Other Gatekeepers," in *Financial Gatekeepers: Can They Protect Investors?*, eds. Yasuyuki Fuchita and Robert E. Litan (Washington, DC: Brookings Institution Press, 2006), 59, 61.

[22] Dylan H. Bruce et al., "Petition for Policy Clarification on Credit Rating Agencies to the Securities and Exchange Commission," Securities & Exchange Commission, January 13, 2023, https://www.sec.gov.

plexity of the analysis being performed, and the principal amount of the issuance."[23] Credit rating agencies make most of their profits from these fees, opening ample space for conflicts of interest (though the agencies are adamant about controlling for this). In the nineties, one Colorado public school district decided to switch from Moody's to S&P Global and Fitch. In retaliation, Moody's issued their own rating, immediately tanking the district's bonds. This was deemed perfectly legal since (astonishingly) credit ratings are considered *opinions* and legally protected by the First Amendment, even when inaccurate or misleading.[24] These opinions have considerable direct material consequences.

To systematically analyze this process, we combined credit ratings from the "Big Three" rating agencies with a government dataset of college-provided data, the Integrated Postsecondary Education Data System (IPEDS).[25] For more information on this data set, analysis, and how to access these data sources, please see Appendix A. Our analysis showed clear evidence of a systemically racist funding stream for higher education in the United States. We found that higher-rated institu-

---

[23] Moody's, "Investors Service Disclosure," Moody's Investors Service, n.d., https://www.moodys.com.

[24] Dori K. Bailey, "The *New York Times* and Credit Rating Agencies: Indistinguishable under First Amendment Jurisprudence," *Denver Law Review* 93, no. 2 (2016): 275–353.

[25] See Appendix A for additional information on the data set, including sources and IPEDS tables used.

tions have more white students and fewer Black and Brown students than lower-rated institutions. This racial hierarchy in credit ratings sits comfortably with racist assumptions about the competence of individuals and institutions assigned different racial identities. In writing about racial capitalism, Jodi Melamed notes that such "fictions of different human capacities" are how "racism enshrines the inequalities that capitalism requires."[26] Here, the fictions of different human capacities meet the fictions of credit rating scores.

We also saw that highly rated institutions have proportionally fewer low-income students, defined as those awarded Pell Grants. The economic stratification of working-class students into lower-rated schools is mirrored by an economic stratification of the schools themselves. Lower-rated schools have fewer financial resources than their higher-rated counterparts, even while paying proportionally more to access institutional debt. Prime-rated institutions (the highest possible rating) have the highest revenues and largest endowments. At the lowest-rated public institutions, endowment holdings averaged just $492 per full-time student and profit margins were close to zero, compared to 30 percent profit margins and $91,800 in endowment per student at the highest-rated public universities. In their 2022 year-end review, S&P Global admitted that "the divide between higher- and

---

[26] Jodi Melamed, "Racial Capitalism," *Critical Ethnic Studies* 1, no. 1 (2015): 76–85.

lower-rated schools continues to widen,"[27] mirroring growing inequalities in individuals' access to credit.

Rating methodology shapes decisions in the higher education industry. According to Sinclair, "Ratings are much more consequential things than they appear behaviorally. They can be likened to federal funding programs in the United States that are conditional on policy change at the state and local level."[28] Higher education institutions must increase their ratings to get better borrowing terms. To increase their ratings, they must implement ever harsher austerity measures and eviscerate any semblance of democratic governance.[29] Better credit ratings track with administrations that can easily raise tuition and fees. As the president of the Council of University of California (UC) Faculty Associations told students amidst a dire financial emergency, "The single most important reason that UC has an excellent bond rating. . . is that it can now raise your tuition at will."[30] From a credit

---

[27] S&P Global Ratings, "U.S. Higher Education 2022 Year In Review," S&P Global Ratings, December 8, 2022, https://www.spglobal.com.

[28] Sinclair, *To the Brink of Destruction*, 30.

[29] This is a general pattern with municipal bonds: higher ratings are actually worse for the public since bondholders and the public have opposing interests; Davon Norris and Elizabeth C. Martin, "Is Good Credit Good? State Credit Ratings and Economic Insecurity, 1996–20121," *Sociological Forum* 37, no. 1 (2022): 246–68.

[30] Bob Meister, "They Pledged Your Tuition," University Council-AFT, n.d., https://ucaft.org.

rating perspective, allowing elected officials to set tuition is more cumbersome—better to have unelected functionaries do it (though, in practice, elected officials tend to do capitalists' bidding). Credit rating agencies prefer for management to have the power to "take decisive actions to preserve fiscal equilibrium."[31] Ironically, these same university managers do not have autonomy from credit rating agencies.

It also helps if the university's governing board is filled with financial experts, not people with educational backgrounds.[32] The chair of the UMass Board of Trustees is also the head of an investment management firm. With a few exceptions, the other trustees are also heads of financial firms. Credit rating firms' criteria for success do not include paying workers fair wages, so drastic pay cuts are rewarded with the highest ratings. Ratings suffer with flexible benefits and labor costs, often derived from faculty governance, state oversight, and a unionized workforce. Therefore, the ability to suppress workers' collective power, crack down on unions, and undermine professors' tenure protections all help. The University of California's massive furloughs of workers in 2009 led to an increase in its bond ratings.[33] This makes institutional debt a

---

[31] Moody's, "Rating Methodology: US Non-for-Profit Private and Public Higher Education," Moody's Investor Service, August 26, 2021, https://ratings.moodys.com.

[32] Eaton, *Bankers in the Ivory Tower.*

[33] Eaton, *Bankers in the Ivory Tower.*

fundamental labor issue; unions are critical sites of struggle against it. Union leadership must embrace the fight against institutional debt and use union resources for research and debt organizing (see the role of the Massachusetts Teachers Association in Chapter 5).

Enrollment growth is another important factor in rating calculations.[34] Colleges and universities are pushed to constantly grow enrollment, mainly by recruiting those most likely to attend full-time (i.e., high school students enrolling right after graduation). This competition for paying customers in state and national student "marketplaces" neglects the potential of local part-time and nontraditional students.[35] Some institutions have recently started to shift more resources into recruiting and retaining nontraditional students; unfortunately, this has been rationalized in the language of the market, customers, and competition, not as access to a public good.[36]

---

[34] Moody's, "Rating Methodology," 13; S&P Global Ratings, "Advancing or Adapting: The State of Play in U.S. Higher Education," S&P Global Ratings, November 29, 2022, https://www.spglobal.com.

[35] Hilary Burns, "Private Colleges Look to Diversify Enrollment by Recruiting Community-College Students," *The Business Journals*, June 24, 2021, https://www.bizjournals.com; Hanover Research, "Strategies for Attracting and Supporting Non-Traditional Students," Highland Community College, January 2018, https://highland.edu.

[36] Janice Hadfield, "Recruiting and Retaining Adult Students," *New Directions for Student Services* 102 (Summer 2003): 17–26.

Lastly, public universities are incentivized to build their brands and spend money on marketing campaigns (e.g., transit advertising, highway billboards, and social media banners). Moody's states this plainly: "A university's ability to shape, protect, and enhance how others perceive the value of its programs and services provides the foundation for its credit rating. Positive indicators of market reputation include: brand identity consistent with the university's mission and market strategies."[37] This disadvantages lower profile local and regional public colleges and universities, which already receive less funding than their flagship counterparts. As Charles Schwab advises investors, "look for educational facilities that have a strong reputation and will continue to attract a large student population."[38] Public research universities focus their marketing and recruitment dollars on out-of-state counties with wealthier, whiter populations to recruit more privileged students who come with higher tuition and test scores.[39]

Encountering glossy advertising campaigns can be jarring for students and workers at underfunded public colleges. For example, students and work-

[37] Moody's, "Rating Methodology. U.S. Not-for-Profit Private and Public Higher Education," The Nacubo Economic Models Project Journey, August 26, 2011, https://emp.nacubo.org.

[38] Cooper Howard, "Choosing Municipal Bonds: GO or Revenue?" Charles Schwab, January 18, 2023, https://www.schwab.com.

[39] Chrystal Han, Ozan Jaquette, and Karina Salazar, "Recruiting the Out-of-State University," *Joyce Foundation Report*, March 2019, https://ozanj.github.io.

ers at Bronx Community College (BCC) might board a bus emblazoned with their institution's ad featuring smiling students, bright indoor college spaces, and the slogan "great programs lead to great careers," meanwhile, BCC had to switch to online instruction in 2022 due to a lack of heat.[40] One might wonder why there is money for advertising but not to keep the college buildings heated in the winter. We know university budgets are complex—the university management did not steal from building maintenance to fund marketing. However, credit ratings certainly incentivize such dubious financial choices.

In the spring of 2020, Moody's downgraded their outlook for the entire US higher education industry from stable to negative as most colleges and universities went online during the COVID-19 pandemic. Moody's noted revenue losses from campus closures, including shuttered dorms, dining halls, parking lots, and athletic facilities.[41] Higher education administrators scrambled to meet bottom lines by furloughing and laying off workers. They also borrowed more, on worse terms, and refinanced their existing debt. Moody's recognized the vicious cycle of lower credit ratings

---

[40] Arrman Kyaw, "Classes Move Online at Bronx Community College Due to Persistent Heating Problems," *Diverse Issues in Higher Education*, November 11, 2022, https://www.diverseeducation.com.

[41] Jeremy Bauer-Wolf, "Moody's Lowers Higher Ed Outlook to Negative amid Coronavirus Crisis," *Higher Ed Dive*, March 18, 2020, https://www.highereddive.com.

and more debt on worse terms: "As the pandemic continues to create a high degree of uncertainty across higher education, there is a rising risk that banks will pull back their exposure to the sector, which would leave many universities with fewer options to mitigate near-term operational stress."[42] In other words, the rating agencies' lower rankings meant that banks would lend on increasingly unfavorable terms. Rather than breaking the puppet master's strings, the pandemic reinforced them. This is common in disaster capitalism, where major disruptions motivate the ramping up of debt and exploitation by financial elites.

In the summer of 2022, dramatic inflation hit the United States. When tuition increases tracked behind inflation, credit rating agencies saw money left on the table.[43] As college workers and students worried about historically high inflation rates, Fitch Ratings bemoaned public institutions' inability to raise tuition without restraint: "While tuition increases at public universities may be necessary to preserve budgetary balance, such increases are often tempered by caps, state approval, and their public mission to keep higher education accessible

---

[42] Moody's, "Higher Education – US 2021 Outlook Negative as Pandemic Weakens Key Revenue Streams," Moody's Investor Service, December 8, 2020, https://www.moodys.com.

[43] Gauri Gupta, "Advancing or Adapting: The State of Play in U.S. Higher Education," S&P Global Ratings, November 29, 2022, https://www.spglobal.com; Moody's, "Higher Education Outlook 2023," Moody's Ratings, December 15, 2022, https://events.moodys.com.

and affordable."[44] Clearly, the credit rating oligopoly sees the public mission of educating people as nothing more than an unfortunate and unprofitable byproduct of the debt university.

OTHER PLAYERS

The following nonexhaustive list reviews some of the other players contributing to the debt economy in higher education.

INSURANCE COMPANIES

Insurance companies are involved in the higher education debt system in their primary capacity (beyond just purchasing municipal bonds). Colleges and universities can improve their credit rating and secure better terms on their debt by beefing up their insurance coverage. Higher education institutions take out different types of insurance for cybersecurity, property, legal liability for their management teams and faculty, and natural disasters. There is also insurance to deal with the financial ramifications of student sexual assault, abusive coaches, campus shootings, and campus protests. During the pandemic, universities were pushed to take on more insurance to cover new cybersecurity risks

---

[44] Fitch Ratings, "Higher Education Tuition Hikes Insufficient to Offset Inflation Pressures," *Fitch Wire*, July 14, 2022, https://www. fitchratings.com.

presented by online learning.[45] Again, local and regional schools find themselves at a disadvantage with insurance terms and rates, miring them further in a cycle of borrowing that deepens class and race inequities. Proliferating insurance also increases the bureaucratic workload for faculty and staff.

FINANCIAL ADVISORS

Financial advisors are well-positioned to help higher education administrators figure out the mess of creditors, underwriters, credit rankings, and insurance companies. A whole class of actors makes money from advising colleges and universities through all these processes and spinning credit strengths to the rating agencies.[46] Financial advisors have rode the larger trend of universities hiring outside consultants—whose expertise in the for-profit sectors is lauded—rather than relying on the experts among their own faculty. The latter, of course, would be more likely to respond to and center the interests of the university community to which they belong.

---

[45] Abi Potter Clough, "How Insurers Are Underwriting Higher Education during the Worst Financial Crisis It's Ever Faced," *Risk and Insurance*, November 23, 2020, https://riskandinsurance.com.

[46] Maxwell Wilkinson, "Review of Rating Agency Outlooks on the Higher Education Sector in 2021," Blue Rose Capital, April 5, 2021, https://www.blueroseadvisors.com.

GOVERNMENT AND GOVERNANCE

The story of institutional debt in higher education is largely the story of defunded public colleges and universities. The move towards debt financing comes with a decline in democratic oversight and governance at public institutions. Private consultants often have more say over how the university operates than democratically elected legislators.

Of course, we should also be critical of the state. In a capitalist society, the government largely protects systems of extraction and disciplines workers. There may be short-term benefits in working with politicians to mitigate harms and expand state funding for public institutions. However, legislators—regardless of party affiliation—serve elite masters, albeit with differing degrees of awareness and enthusiasm. The defunding of public institutions and subsequent push toward debt financing has been a bipartisan project to help the wealthy accumulate ever more wealth. Even the rosy memory of "fully funded" higher education was characterized by the racist exclusion of working-class students of color and settler enrichment from the theft of Indigenous land.[47]

More complete governance of our public colleges and universities by the state does not solve the problems of governance by financial elites (not least because, in a capitalist system, governments and financial elites are not distinct). We do not

---

[47] Robert Lee et al., "Land-Grab Universities: A High Country News Investigation," *High Country News*, March 2020, https://www.landgrabu.org.

necessarily want more financial oversight by legislators. After all, the government pushed public colleges and universities into debt, legally enforced the terms of the debt, and repeatedly bailed out bankers to reward theft and corruption. University governance should be bottom up—by the students, workers, and communities. This requires a deep and wide democratic structure for popular deliberation over how public funding is spent, with faculty and staff unions and student organizations at the table. This vision of bottom-up governance is showcased in the proposal developed by the Multisectoral Commission for University Reform at the University of Puerto Rico (see Chapter 6).[48]

SETTING THE STAGE FOR CAMPUS DEBT

Public college and university borrowing provides tremendous opportunities for private investors and financial players to enrich themselves. The costs are borne by students, faculty and staff, public institutions, and their communities. Colleges borrow increasing amounts to make up for government shortfalls, meaning more and more of their budgets are allocated to pay debt interest and fees. In 2020, public university interest payments totaled $7.7 billion, with significant variation in debt burdens across types of colleges.[49] In the words of

---

[48] Rima Brusi and Isar Godreau, "Public Higher Education in Puerto Rico: Disaster, Austerity, and Resistance," *AAUP Journal of Academic Freedom* 12 (2021): 1–19.

[49] U.S. Department of Education, National Center for Education Statistics, Integrated Postsecondary Education Data

Fred Moten and Stefano Harney, the university has become a "credential granting front for finance capitalism and a machine for stratification."[50]

Colleges are bound by debt covenants—the legal agreements stipulating conditions of borrowing. These covenants bind institutions to private banks, undermining or even severing their obligation to students, workers, and communities. While the use of "*covenant*" might imply mutual agreement, the reality of these debt covenants necessarily reflects power hierarchies. Higher education borrowers agree to repay the debt using almost any type of revenue. For example, creditors in Massachusetts can intercept state funding for the nine public state colleges if there are no other funds to ensure timely full payments.[51] The public university is first and foremost responsible to its creditors, so it prioritizes payments above basic survival (let alone the flourishing of students and workers). Debt payments supersede payroll and health insurance for the workers, financial aid for students, and basic health and safety provisions amidst pandemics and

---

System (IPEDS), 2021 "F2021_F1A" (finance) table. Retrieved from https://nces.ed.gov/ipeds/datacenter/InstitutionByName.aspx on November 28, 2022. This amount is calculated from IPEDS' data on interest expenses in the "F2021_F1A" (finance) table, adjusted to November 2022 values.

[50] Fred Moten and Stefano Harvey, "The University: Last Words," *FUC YouTube*, July 9, 2020, https://www.youtube.com.

[51] Massachusetts State College Building Authority, *Financial Statements (With Supplementary Information) and Independent Auditor's Reports* (Boston: Cohn & Reznick, 2019), 15.

climate collapse. Covenants bind the duty of the university to bankers, not to the people.

Institutional debt further entrenches inequalities in the public higher education landscape. The most disadvantaged college students are least likely to graduate, partly because they attend segregated, defunded institutions and are taught and advised by the most exploited workers. These institutions also contend with the worst credit ratings and borrowing conditions. Colleges at the bottom of the hierarchy face *predatory inclusion* (to borrow a term from Louise Seamster and Raphaël Charron-Chénier). Borrowing allows them to continue functioning, but the very conditions of their inclusion into the higher education industry jeopardize their long-term purpose.[52] They do not have endowments, major donors, or competitive athletic programs. Rather, these institutions pass the debt onto their students through tuition and fees, exacerbating the inequities these students already face. Increasingly, nonelite public colleges exist in a perpetual crisis mode. William Paterson University in New Jersey responded to a multimillion-dollar deficit in 2021 by shuttering majors and laying off a third of its professors. Similarly, New Jersey City University closed over a third of its programs and laid off faculty to balance the budget. Both colleges

---

[52] Louise Seamster and Raphaël Charron-Chénier, "Predatory Inclusion and Education Debt: Rethinking the Racial Wealth Gap," *Social Currents* 4, no. 3 (2017): 199–207.

disproportionately serve first-generation, working-class students of color.[53]

Campus activists fighting against austerity rarely discuss the debt economy in higher education. Our ire is often directed at greedy campus administrators and coaches with ballooning salaries and golden parachutes. We fight adjunctification, pay cuts, and layoffs, but rarely does our analysis extend beyond state-level budget cuts. We lose the threads that harness public colleges and universities to the imperative to produce profit and enrich the elites.

This chapter offered a fresh set of targets and a new battle terrain beyond university administrators and boards of trustees. These targets go beyond symptoms to get to the root of the problem. Understanding the players within the higher education debt system is the first step in breaking the debt machine. As in the *Grapes of Wrath*, we can identify the agents of something that "isn't a man at all." We take to heart Mario Savio's 1964 exhortation: "There is a time when the operation of the machine becomes so odious, makes you so sick at heart, that you can't take part; you can't even passively take part, and you've got to put your bodies upon the gears and upon the wheels, upon the levers, upon all the apparatus, and you've got to make it stop. And you've got to indicate to the people who run it, to the people who own it, that

---

[53] Liam Knox, "A Push for More Oversight of New Jersey's Colleges," *Inside Higher Ed*, January 26, 2023, https://www.inside-highered.com.

unless you're free, the machine will be prevented from working at all!"[54]

It is demoralizing that our public campuses are indebted to funds, trusts, banks, and corporations. How can we hold these actors accountable? On the road to debt abolition, we envision fighting for short-term harm reduction reforms: suspending payments, lowering interest rates and fees, and deprioritizing loan repayments. While reforms alone cannot destroy the status quo, they lessen the pain born by students, workers, and communities in the higher education debt economy.

---

[54] Michael Jackman, "Mario Savio's 'bodies upon the gears' speech – 50 years later," *Detroit Metro Times*, December 1, 2014, https://www.metrotimes.com/news/mario-savios-bodies-upon-the-gears-speech-50-years-later-2271095.

CHAPTER THREE
WHY WE NEED TO ORGANIZE
AGAINST CAMPUS DEBT
(EVEN THOUGH IT'S DIFFICULT)
AND HOW TO BEGIN

This chapter discusses the importance of bottom-up organizing to build power against campus debt. Campus debt presents organizing challenges, as it is more obscure, opaque, and frequently obtuse than student loan debt. Furthermore, in the hyper-individualistic and consumeristic framework of this neoliberal era, campus debt is seen (when it is seen) as less clearly and directly linked to us as individuals. This makes collective action difficult but not impossible![1]

There are many reasons to organize *urgently* before campuses incur even more debt. Students must borrow to pay for both campus operational costs and campus debt, frequently working mul-

---

[1] Mancur Olson, Jr., *The Logic of Collective Action: Public Goods and the Theory of Groups* (Cambridge: Harvard University Press, 1971).

tiple jobs to do so.[2] Therefore, cancelling campus debt could reduce student loan totals. As demonstrated in Chapter 1 and 2, campus debt also affects education quality, as it is prioritized over educational expenditure. Campus debt de-democratizes public universities, so cancelling it will reduce the financiers' roles and interest in our campus communities. Because debt oppresses so many, it offers a widely relatable access point for bringing us together to undo the system. Revealing the sources of campus debt and the harm it causes can unite people who would otherwise not come together. Finally, given that hopes for cancelling student loan debt were raised and crushed, this may be a particularly good point in time for organizing around another form of educational debt.

In what follows, we explore the types of organizing needed to fight debt, highlighting obstacles you may face and considering how to overcome them. To do this, we draw on lessons learned from the Debt Collective, experiences organizing against

---

[2] One of the main—and flawed—arguments made to the Supreme Court against student loan forgiveness was that it would undermine states' ability to pay campus debt. See Thomas Gokey, Eleni Schirmer, Braxton Brewington, and Louise Seamster, "The Suit against Student Debt Relief Doesn't Add Up: Flawed Claims of Legal Standing in Biden v. Nebraska," *Roosevelt Institute*, May 2, 2023, https://rooseveltinstitute.org; Ayelet Sheffey, "Why a Federal Court Blocked Biden's Student-Debt Cancellation Even after a Major Loan Company Undermined a Key Argument in the GOP-Led Lawsuit," *Business Insider*, November 15, 2022, https://www.businessinsider.com; Michael Stratford, "The Student Loan Company Being Used to Attack Biden's Debt Relief Plan," *Politico*, December 17, 2022, https://www.politico.com.

campus debt at Salem State University, and discussions about campus debt organizing within *Labor Notes'* Public Higher Education Workers (PHEW) network.

BUILDING THE POWER TO FIGHT CAMPUS DEBT

The real work underpinning political change does not rely on petitioning and government officials. Rather, organizing, power-building, and movements change the conversation, pressure public officials/leaders, and enact direct forms of action and transformation. This kind of organizing, as Jane McAlevey notes, needs to reach beyond your already convinced followers.[3] It helps people to better understand how an issue affects them (and those they do not know but who are also important). Such organizing is counterhegemonic, meaning it challenges the legitimacy of existing political, economic, and cultural structures. It even has the potential to be radically transformative (see Chapters 4–6 for examples).

The work of the Debt Collective,[4] which evolved out of Occupy Wall Street, demonstrates that such bottom-up organizing is doable and provides many potential paths and lessons for organizing against campus debt. When the Debt Collective started,

---

[3] Jane F. McAlevey, *No Shortcuts: Organizing for Power* (New York: Oxford University Press, 2016), 11–12.

[4] See https://debtcollective.org/.

student loan debt cancellation was perceived as an impossible and utopian demand. Indeed, it took years of political education organizing—at the local and national levels—to lay the basis for future victories. This education helped people understand how student debt worked, its economics, and its underlying social and ethical immorality. The Debt Collective slowly began to change the narrative on student loan debt, reframing heroes and villains.

The Debt Collective strategically picked particularly vulnerable targets and winnable struggles. For example, they pushed the Obama administration to create a simple tool to help students defend against predatory lending. The "Corinthian 15" debt strike against a for-profit higher education institution—known for "unconscionably. . . target[ing] low-income workers, single parents and veterans"—led to $5.8 billion in automatic student loan forgiveness.[5] That strike would not have happened without the Debt Collective. These wins helped to put the Debt Collective on the political map. Now, student loan debt cancellation is no longer seen as impossible; it is a central issue in the US political economy. Importantly, the Debt Collective framed student loan debt not only as an economic issue but also *as a moral and ethical issue*. They followed the Zapatista motto of "going slow because we are going far." In other words, they committed to a

---

[5] Stacey Cowley, "$5.8 Billion in Loans Will Be Forgiven for Corinthian Colleges Students," *New York Times*, June 1, 2022, https://www.nytimes.com.

long-term struggle, based on bottom-up organizing, to transform the structures of society, not only to receive immediate relief. Most recently, this organizing forced the Biden Administration to put forward its limited and unsuccessful student loan debt relief plan.

OBSTACLES TO ORGANIZING AGAINST CAMPUS DEBT

Debt—particularly campus debt—is relatively opaque, a consciously veiled oppressive force. It doesn't hit people in the face. It still flies below the radar of popular and academic culture. It is less blatant than some other forms of oppression, with less obvious collective and individual damage inflicted. As organizers from within, we use various forms of "reveals"—a people's form of auditing—to clarify what campus debt is and its direct and indirect, individual and collective consequences. We also strategically organize around debt by helping people understand how it is linked to wider social trends and structures and how they can intervene to make positive short-term and structural changes.

Austerity is key to understanding these overall trends: by constantly raising tuition and fees to compensate for reductions in taxes for the wealthy, austerity makes public higher education less accessible and thus reduces the number of students; and, equally, by reducing campus budgets, it reduces the number of higher education workers and intensifies working and learning conditions. While this can make it harder to organize on campuses, understanding austerity allows us to ground our findings and our fight within a broader context. However, the word "austerity" can be daunting; we often prefer not to use it—rather, we demonstrate what austerity is, how it works, and how it affects people. Debt is a form of discipline—frequently presented in terms of "accountability"—imposed on the resources, time, and very lives of working people/the less powerful. Debt is both an economic and power relationship that extracts resources and wealth from one class and gives it to another (thereby exacerbating preexisting economic, racial, and gender inequalities). It increases the ruling class' wealth and control at the expense of the rest of us.

Once people understand how debt and austerity affect them, they can become more active. When Vanessa Bramante, a recent graduate of Salem State, learned that around $17,000 of her tuition and fees went toward campus debt, she reflected on how these previously unknown payments had stolen her time:

> That should be something you are told upfront. That's nearly 50 percent of my undergrad student loan debt. . . . I worked two mindless jobs junior and senior year and lost out on social opportunities. After classes, I went straight to work. After work, I crammed for tests and did assignments. . . . I was over-extended. But without a college degree, your

options are limited, so you have to pick up odd jobs like that. I didn't get a chance to meet people and do all things on campus.

Another student, Gayathri Raja, a sophomore at UMass Lowell, who participated in revealing campus debt reflected:

> Before I was involved with this project, I had been completely unaware that campus debt even existed and of the impact it has on students, faculty, resources, and the quality of our education. . . . Diving into the financials of our state colleges and speaking to many of the parties involved has opened my eyes to the danger of this immense amount of debt existing and how it is largely concealed from the public. The changes in public higher education and its funding that this project is fighting for attacks the problems at the source.

A key challenge in organizing around campus debt is that people have extremely limited time. Higher education workers frequently cannot pursue activities beyond their immediate work demands, likely due to constant speed-ups and workload increases driven by austerity and the need to pay their own student loan debt. Students also have their education sabotaged and time "stolen" by debt (in being forced to work multiple jobs to pay for school). This downward spiral must be broken:

debt steals time that workers and students need to fight against debt (and other forms of oppression).

We frequently heard that many people were uninterested in or apathetic towards the "politics" of their institution, including being involved in the union or political activism. This "apathy" is frequently the result of many other determining factors, such as being overworked or scared. For instance, a growing number of tenure-track (and even tenured) workers now fear losing their jobs (a fear that has long affected adjuncts and staff) and feel hopeless or directionless.[6] Many others are burnt out by ongoing negative local, national, and global political trends. Trumpism, white nationalism, overt racism, climate change, and attacks on reproductive justice and LGTBQ+ rights are all demoralizing. One-on-one conversations in the spring of 2020 revealed that most faculty at Salem State were experiencing significant emotional distress, including feelings of helplessness, frustration, demoralization, and exhaustion from being negated, undervalued, and dismissed. Few could rise for active resistance at that moment, but over time, the number of members willing to demonstrate, write letters, and attend meetings grew; this provided hope and solidarity for others.

Another challenge is that many academic workers—particularly professors—see themselves as professionals with a direct, individual relationship

---

[6] Labor Notes Staff, "Beating Apathy," *Labor Notes*, December 15, 2015, https://www.labornotes.org.

with the university, not as workers with shared issues and interests. They frequently do not identify with other campus workers and tend to stay at a distance from union and campus organizing. Furthermore, many unions would not see organizing against campus debt as within their scope. These top-down "business unions" refuse to address key political issues (or only do so behind closed doors), further reinforcing apathy, passivity, and perceived helplessness.

Another obstacle to organizing is the pervasive common sense about debt. Its many narratives suggest that debtors, both individuals and campuses, choose to take out loans and have an ethical obligation to pay them back; it also positions debt as an effective way to resolve financial problems, an inevitability, or a profitable venture. This framework neglects the nature of debt as a *power relationship used to discipline workers*. This logic also ignores more fundamental questions like why so many people's incomes are so low that they need to borrow from powerful private institutions to get by? As *Labor Notes* quips, "People do not live beyond their means. They are *denied* the means to live." Not challenging this framework means accepting the immoral and irrational framework and madness of capitalism.

Finally, it can be intimidating to scan through financial documents. They are not easy to read and are not designed for analyzing campus debt and its consequences. They are supposed to track the institution's financial position, cash flow, and budgetary compliance to determine the institution's ability to meet its obligations (i.e., debt payments). These are not objective documents; they reflect political, educational, and moral choices (e.g., what is prioritized for funding and what is prioritized for cuts). Their language, categories, and terms can be opaque and inconsistent across (or even within) states.[7]

OVERCOMING THE OBSTACLES IN PRACTICE

Organizing always needs to address the circumstances of individual campuses. Each campus and/or system needs to determine the most pressing issues that will galvanize their colleagues to build power and collectively challenge debt. For example, at Salem State, pandemic-related threats of layoffs, furloughs, reduced classes, majors and programs, and even retrenchment[8] were a unifying trigger for

---

[7] These reports are written to conform to governmental accounting standards which purportedly are "intended to promote financial reporting that provides useful information to taxpayers, public officials, investors, and others who use financial reports" (Government Accounting Standards Board, "About the GASB," *Government Accounting Standards Board*, n.d., https://www.gasb.org/, para. 2). However, the financial reports are really meant for investors and governmental oversight entities (Integrated Postsecondary Education Data System, "Use the Data," *Integrated Postsecondary Education Data System*, n.d., https://nces.ed.gov/ipeds/) rather than taxpayers and the university community. Variations within these standards make the reports more or less transparent (e.g., how off-book debt taken on through third parties like state building authorities is reported).

[8] Salem State University Board of Trustees, "Board of Trustees Meeting Minutes," *Salem State University*, June 10, 2020, https://www.salemstate.edu

faculty and students. This forced us to look into the factors causing the dire situation.

We determined that campus debt—some 10 percent of the SSU budget—and not small classes or overpaid workers was the source of the crisis. In short, students were sent home during the pandemic, so student residence fees plummeted. Salem State's trustees had pledged dorm revenues to pay the debt service on bonds taken out for these buildings. Now, they needed to find millions to make up the deficit. Per state law and bond agreements, debt payments must take priority over educational expenses. The proposed cuts to the campus operational budget were "needed" to service these debt payments.

This was the first time we ever considered campus debt and its centrality to the crisis and the future of Salem State. After this, we began to consciously organize against campus debt. We built on preexisting organizing to start a campus debt reveal, including a teach-in about the real reasons for the perpetual financial crisis and a campus unity campaign.[9] We started with a small group of people interested in finding out how much debt our campus had, what it was for, and how it affected education at SSU. The group, made up of both faculty and students, did not include any economics or financial specialists. However, having

---

[9] Rich Levy and Joanna Gonsalves, "Our Faculty Union Exposed the University's Debt—And Who's Paying for It," *Labor Notes*, August 26, 2020, https://labornotes.org; This article is a fuller exposition of our organizing.

people from different fields and experiences broadened and deepened our analysis. It also proved that campus finances need not be intimidating: all campus members can and should understand university finances.

Examining how organizing against campus debt could improve students' education linked student experiences to the working conditions of tenure track, non-tenure track and adjunct faculty, librarians, and staff (whether in unions or not), and the collapsing campus infrastructure. We found that reducing (or even eliminating) campus debt payments would not completely resolve these issues. However, savings could lead to tuition and fee reductions and/or educationally motivated spending decisions. In other words, reducing or eliminating campus debt frees up resources that can be redirected into building the type of public higher education and campuses we desire. The Debt Reveal Toolkit[10] and, specifically, the Debt Reveal Worksheet, helped us calculate the debt on campus and envision alternative ways to spend the money (Appendix B).

Collectively engaging in these debt reveal activities pushed us to question how other elements of campus organization and structure might lead to crisis. There were the common culprits of excessive salaries, staffing, and programs and inevitably declining enrollment. Others on and

---

[10] "Debt Audit Tool Kit," n.d., *The *Other* College Debt Crisis*, https://salemmscadocs.home.blog.

off campus argued that administrative bloat was the main financial problem. The increase in upper administration and institutional support roles is frequently attributed to the additional tracking and "accountability'"required by credit agencies and the government, as well as the corporatization of higher education.[11] While this is a significant problem, our organizing and research at Salem State revealed that campus debt payments are usually much more significant than higher administration positions and salaries (roughly 10 percent of the budget went to debt; only 3 percent was for administrative bloat).[12]

Our organizing helped workers and students see that campus debt is but one form of public-sector institutional debt that pervades all parts of our lives. For instance, austerity has also forced increased prices, service cutbacks, and worse working conditions in the public transportation sector. Inadequate funding for public transportation and infrastructure results in crumbling roads and bridges, the privatization of roads and parking, higher tolls, worse working conditions, and a less green society.[13] Debt also undermines PreK–12

---

[11] Thomas Wesley Williamson, E. Shannon Hughes, and Penny L. Head, "An Exploration of Administrative Bloat in American Higher Education," *Planning for Higher Education Journal* 46, no. 2 (2018): 15–22.

[12] CTHRU Statewide Payroll, "Payroll Summary 2023," *CTHRU Statewide Payroll*, n.d., https://cthrupayroll.mass.gov.

[13] Donald Cohen and Allen Mikaelian, *The Privatization of Everything: How the Plunder of Public Goods Transformed America and*

education; it is cited as an excuse to close schools, particularly in minority areas in Chicago, and even to undermine school lunches. Austerity and debt turn the world upside down.[14] Linking campus debt to other people's lived experiences creates a basis for alliances with unions and off-campus community organizations (see Chapter 6 for on-and-off-campus links in organizing against debt in Puerto Rico).

TAKEAWAYS: OVERCOMING OBSTACLES IN ORGANIZING

The following pages present key lessons from our organizing around this issue and the Debt Collective's organizing around student loan debt. History teaches us that organizing around debt and labor issues can build power and create change.

How We Can Fight Back (New York: New Press, 2023); Donald Cohen and Stephanie Farmer, "Why Chicago's Botched Parking Meter Privatization Is Also Bad for the Environment," *Next City*, June 4, 2014, https://nextcity.org.

[14] In an amazing example of how the system protects the investments of our financial overlords, "the Biden administration's Securities and Exchange Commission is suing the City of Rochester, NY, contending that 'rampant overspending on teacher salaries' plunged the city's school district into 'extreme financial distress,' misleading investors who bought municipal bonds." Ira Stoll, "Biden Administration Sues a City Over 'Rampant Overspending on Teacher Salaries,'" *Education Next*, June 15, 2022, https://www.educationnext.org.

DON'T GET BOGGED DOWN IN THE RESEARCH

Never forget that your campus debt project is primarily an *organizing project*, not a research project. The data is not an end in itself. The analysis needs to be thorough enough to be dangerous and for us to organize, but it is not a detailed academic study. You do not want to hire an "expert" to do the research. This alienates us from the information and disempowers us. Awareness is only the first step in organizing and mobilizing people around campus debt. Debt reveals have illuminated well-hidden and outrageous realities. This new information frequently infuriates both those doing the collective research and those learning about it later. The conclusions we have reached and published are in line with in-depth research on this topic.[15]

Remember, while good arguments based on the debt reveal are critical for building our base, most decision-makers will not be convinced to change their positions by good arguments alone. Therefore, debt reveals must be part of organizing so we can bring organized power (e.g., coalitions, demonstrations, withholding labor, and/or various forms of electoral power) to bear on the university and/or college, system administrations, and state and local governments.

---

[15] Charlie Eaton, *Bankers in the Ivory Tower: The Troubling Rise of Financiers in US Higher Education* (Chicago: Chicago University Press, 2022), 99, 106–8, 126–7.

BUILD ALLIANCES

Start with a small group on your campus, then expand to other campus groups. Later, seek alliances with groups at other institutions or even national campaigns. Campus debt is not merely an economic issue—it has moral, ethical, social, wellness, and environmental ramifications (e.g., it affects funding for mental health counseling and safe and green buildings). Your group should be as *interdisciplinary and cross-experiential* as possible. Different perspectives can only add range and depth to your analysis.

Starting with a small group does not mean isolating yourself until you reach a certain degree of success. The authors of this book came together after hearing about debt work on other campuses in *Labor Notes*' Public Higher Education Workers (PHEW) meetings. Once we got started, we held national online workshops and outreach programs to provide ongoing support and skill-building for individuals at universities across the country. Look for such networks. They can help you share learning and experience, understand differences between states and political units, and grasp the national structures that underpin campus debt.

One-on-one conversations are an important part of organizing and building alliances. They allow organizers to really understand people's concerns, link them to campus debt and allied issues, and generate interest in joining or staying involved in the work. To be clear, one-on-one conversations are a key method for organizing ourselves. They should *never* be used when dealing with your campus administration; individuals/officials/leaders should never meet with the administration alone.[16] Always go with a group.

CAMPUS DEBT IS A LABOR ISSUE

Campus debt is a labor issue that reinforces austerity, downsizing, speed-ups, and reductions in wages and benefits. Worker organizations and unions can and must play a major role in showcasing how different forms of debt (even beyond the sphere of the campus) reinforce one another to steal time and labor power from working people in all spheres of life. This can help people go beyond individualistic perspectives and begin to see their common interests. They can then deploy collective power to resist austerity, force change, and improve working and learning conditions. When well-organized, we can selectively (work to rule) or fully (strike) withhold labor. We must bring our unions and worker organizations to this struggle and integrate it into other labor issues.

This comes with (at least) two caveats. Firstly, not all unions support bottom-up organizing. Building democratic, member-driven unions is a parallel and

---

[16] Meeting individually with management not only involves a power imbalance, but such conversations isolate leaders from their base. In addition, as Salem State's experience has shown, such conversations can compromise those leaders when they are asked (or demands are made) to keep certain conversations secret. This is a *de facto* alignment with management and alienation from the members.

overlapping task to resisting debt (see guidance in *Labor Notes*). You do not need a member-driven democratic union to start organizing and may initially have to organize against debt around or outside of your union's formal structure. This kind of bottom-up participatory organizing can even help to build such a union. Secondly, organizing around campus debt can also occur beyond unions. Student government organizations, informal student groups, community groups, and alumni organizations can all support such organizing, particularly if you link the struggle to wider issues (e.g., minimum wage, racial equity). Campus debt organizing must remain focused on long-term movement building and the small steps and victories (and setbacks) that build collective action and power.

DON'T FORGET THE STUDENTS

Students are the reason we teach, and building alliances with them is a long-term process, not a last-minute request. It is critical to frame our demands in terms of student interests—reducing student debt, fighting austerity, and improving working conditions to improve learning conditions. This keeps us focused on our goals and undermines the argument that we are solely and/or selfishly fighting for our self-interest. The slogan "our working conditions are our students' learning conditions" articulates this clearly and resonates with many.

Reaching out to busy students can be complex. It is much easier to approach student organizations if you have ongoing relationships, developed outside of classes, and support their needs and demands. Addressing key political and funding issues in classes you teach can lead to accusations of using your (grading) power to manipulate students. A student might complain that the discussion was biased or manipulative. Then, the administration could exaggerate and manipulate this incident to attack you individually and organizationally (as happened at Salem State). Potential responses to such attacks include appeals for academic freedom and the need to discuss critical issues in education. It may also be useful to look for cases of right-wing speech or positions put forward by the administration that offended some students and public higher education workers but did not generate any response or discipline. Such appeals to fairness are not likely to sway our opponents, but they can be useful for organizing and mobilizing students and higher education workers.

RECOGNIZE PEOPLE'S WORK

This helps address some of the overload people face when their time is stolen to pay debt. Recognition can be support and appreciation (e.g., participants get to co-sign on works created) or financial and institutional (e.g., paid time off for hourly staff for participation in this work, formal recognition in job performance evaluations). Provide stipends, internships, and/or course credit for students when possible. At a minimum, support your students by using these experiences to strengthen their resumes.

Remember that creating awareness and understanding campus debt is only the first step in mobilizing and organizing against it. The steps and tactics we outline in this book are only examples, not blueprints. Each campus will be different. We hope you will adapt and expand upon these methods.

PREPARE TO CONFRONT YOUR OPPONENTS

You will confront numerous strategies, tactics, accusations, and threats from the administration. It is important to be prepared. While your opponents are frequently sophisticated and wield formidable bureaucratic, financial, and personnel power, never underestimate their ability to make stupid decisions. For example, at Salem State, for the first time in history, the board did not approve recommendations for tenure and promotion, arguing that it did not have enough clarity on the budget due to the pandemic. This was patently absurd since the cost of tenure and promotions was minuscule—about .001 percent of the total budget. However, this attack led to an unprecedented 200 faculty and librarians attending the board meeting; board members began to backtrack the very next day.

Similarly, because their perspective is so different from ours, they sometimes proudly publish outrageous information that infuriates workers, students, and community members. For example, Salem State publicly reported that the average full-time equivalent (FTE) student would pay $2,960 toward debt servicing in FY2019.[17] The administration assumed this would assuage bondholders but never considered how students or educators would react. Never miss an opportunity to use such situations—they come in campus emails, administration press releases, official reports, board meeting documents, and even orally. The Salem State administration also accidentally allowed a secret potential retrenchment list to become public. It included some 10 percent of tenured liberal arts faculty along with individual names, departments, and proposals (e.g., switch department, remove). This created opportunities for organizing since both the secrecy of the process and the content of the proposal infuriated faculty and, to a lesser extent, students who would have more limited educational opportunities.

Prepare to be accused of incivility when directly confronting incorrect or false narratives and bad policies. This can come from the administration, union leadership,[18] or even union/community members. When we posted a picture of the president with the subtitle "Stop Gutting Salem State," we were attacked for being uncivil, but the action emboldened us and increased our support. In the fight against the debt-related furloughs, workers peacefully occupied the presidential suite. This

---

[17] Salem State University, "Ratio Calculations & Other Measurements," *Salem State University*, June 30, 2019, https://www.salem-state.edu

[18] Remember, sometimes when you aim at the boss/administration, you hit the (bad) union leadership.

too was criticized by some as uncivil, but it also increased activism. Playing nice doesn't always work.

Prepare to be told that personal relationships, private meetings, and backdoor negotiations are better than building power through transparency and (member) participation. In the best-case scenario, you can point to cases in which building and using power against opponents (and even being "uncivil") have led to victories at the campus, system, or statewide level. You may also point to specific cases where the personal relations/backdoor approach failed. While organizing against the furloughs at SSU, the statewide leadership of the faculty/librarian union, the Massachusetts State College Association (MSCA), asked members to rely on the leadership's "expert knowledge" to resolve the crisis rather than organizing or even mobilizing. The union leadership's secret negotiations completely failed, ending with the union waiving its right to bargain or challenge the furloughs. To navigate around "business union" structures that restricted communication *among* members, Salem State workers created a new email list called *The Watercooler,* where all union members could post their thoughts and directly respond to one another. We also created online messaging channels so that members could immediately react and communicate during board or administration-run webinars.

As you gain power, prepare to be kept out of key administrative meetings, discussions, and venues.

Two methods may help here. First, create enough outside pressure—petitions, demonstrations, social media, emails, letters to the editor and op-eds, internal organizing, and communication among members—that it becomes difficult for the administration to push the issue to the side. Second, alliances with students can be crucial since many administrators tend to publicly disrespect students less than workers.

Workers must be prepared to be threatened with job loss or promotion and tenure denial, and students should be prepared to be denied certain rights and privileges. Utilize all contractual and legal avenues to protect yourself, workers, and students. Importantly, never rely exclusively on secretive and individualistic processes. Publicize and organize around the threats to academic freedom and the notion of public higher education as a public good.

Be prepared for campus administrations to consciously pit higher education workers with different job classifications and protections against one another. At Salem State, the administration attempted to create inter-union conflict and distrust by portraying the faculty/librarian union as selfish for fighting against the furloughs, while the staff union and AFSCME (American Federation of State, County, and Municipal Employees representing administrative aides, custodians, trade workers, and campus police) were portrayed as good for negotiating and accepting the furloughs. In reality, the other two unions had no tenure and fewer job protections and were in a weaker position to negotiate. However, this tactic succeeded in creating a poor working relationship among the unions, a wound that has only recently begun to heal.

Be prepared to be pitted against students and their families. The university president came to a student government meeting and threatened that students would face massive fee increases without five weeks of furloughs for all campus workers.[19] Students correctly saw this as an attempt to undermine their education and spontaneously created petitions signed by thousands of students opposing these actions.[20, 21] We supported students both in clarifying the issue and in fighting for their causes:

---

[19] The president's threats were not associated with the process for raising tuition and fees, although most students did not know this. Ultimately, all campus workers suffered a two-week furlough and about 25 percent of adjuncts were laid off. The financial "savings" from these furloughs (some $3.3 million, of which $1.5 million came from MSCA members—faculty and librarians) were not the key to resolving the financial crisis. Rather, restructuring the university's capital debt saved some $11 million in 2021 (highlighting the centrality of this debt to the university's structural financial crisis). State and federal COVID-19 funds were also used. In 2023, furloughed workers were given a small monetary compensation and additional personal days to redress the furloughs. See Dustin Luca, "Salem State imposes furloughs for faculty, librarians," *Salem News*, March 9, 2021, https://www.salemnews.com/; Salem State University, "SSU Fy22 All Funds Budget," *Salem State University*, June 2, 2021, https://records.salemstate.edu.

[20] These petitions were collectively signed by over 3,000 students. Olivia Setzer, "Tell SSU that Students Need Their Professors," *Change.org*, November 25, 2020, https://www.change.org.

[21] Thea Louise, "Petition to Stop the Furloughs," *Change.org*, March 7, 2021, https://www.change.org.

a pass/no pass grading policy for the semester, reimbursement for unused meal and dorm fees, and for the university to champion federal and state proposals for financial relief. We also supported them when they called for student, faculty, and staff input on decisions affecting SSU's future, special consideration for survivors of sexual violence, and for non-union dining hall staff to be rehired.[22]

Be prepared to be criticized and attacked for not being informed, being naive, and having errant figures. We suggest always being clear on what you are claiming, understating your claims, and using rounded numbers to minimize such attacks. Such attacks can come from those who accept common sense about debt. For example, an administrator at Framingham State University wrote a detailed (and condescending) email in response to a debt reveal student team member's request for information:

> To be frank, this exercise—as described—appears to be more of a political call for increased support (a good thing) not an overly sophisticated analysis of institutional debt and its impact on students. . . . The Commonwealth does not subsidize residence hall operations so the costs have to be covered from rent (just as if students were to reside at a private apartment building—that would

---

[22] Levy and Gonsalves, "Our Faculty Union Exposed the University's Debt."

also be pricing to generate a profit)[23]. . . . I also have issues with the premise that debt "is bad". . . debt is an effective financing tool. To again use the Hemenway Lab example, FSU— having decided that the additional scope was beneficial to students (even recognizing the additional costs)—could have funded the noted $15M contribution out of reserves instead of taking on additional debt. Instead, it elected to maintain those funds in investment accounts that have returned over 9 percent on average over the past decade while our annual interest costs through borrowing was closer to 3 percent (and our recent debt restructuring brought those interest rate costs down to 1.75 percent). . . . That is, [the] use of debt—in this case—has had a very favorable impact on student costs as these investment returns are subsidizing general operations.

Numerous "common sense" assumptions about debt and reserves are embedded in this response. Such statements can be very frustrating and/or unnerving for students and/or higher education workers. They rely on the neoliberal notion that public higher education institutions should make profits like private enterprises ("good" borrowing will be profitable) and that large reserves are

---

[23] Arguing that pricing for dorms would parallel the private market eliminates the distinction between public and private goods, as neoliberalism often does.

both necessary and good. This common sense also obscures underlying unequal power relationships.

So, be prepared to refute these claims. For example, if public higher education were adequately funded, there would be no need for loans to build dorms nor for dorm costs to mirror the private market.[24] Large reserves (investment accounts and cash reserves) would also be obsolete without the need to secure a good credit rating and address cash shortfalls.[25] We must ask whether reserves come from student fees and, if so, why student fees were high enough to allow the development of large reserves. When can reserves be used; if they are for emergencies, how are emergencies defined and by whom? Notably, when higher education workers pressured the UMass board of trustees to use the reserves to avoid cutbacks during COVID-19, "member Michael O'Brien. . . said an emergency use of the system's cash reserves would be for an unforeseen catastrophe, such as an asteroid hitting the earth."[26]

---

[24] 60 percent of average dorm rent from Massachusetts state universities went to debt service, while deposits went to reserves; see the "Massachusetts State College Building Authority, Annual Report Fiscal 2020."

[25] Certainly, given the ebb and flow of enrollment and other factors (even in normal times), some cash reserves (and/or a letter of credit) can be necessary.

[26] Bera Dunau and Scott Merzbach, "UMass Unions Protest Job Cuts, Furloughs," *Daily Hampshire Gazette*, March 8, 2021, https://www.gazettenet.com.

If you are at a campus with a large endowment, be prepared to respond to statements that your campus does not need more state funding. One response to this is that endowments are most frequently restricted by donors and cannot be used for operating expenditures.[27] Be prepared to counter these attacks by changing the paradigm as well. For example, ask whether the resources and energy that many public campuses put into raising private funds to build reserves and endowments is an efficient use of resources. What are the costs of this fundraising? How much of a useful return do they bring in, given that only endowment earnings (usually in the 4–5 percent range) can be spent? Would the time and resources spent raising private funds not be better spent attempting to increase public funding, which would likely generate far more spendable money in both the short and longer term?

---

[27] Reserves and endowments are different. Reserves are funds needed for regular cash flow fluctuations. Endowments consist of private donations (and income generated from them). Usually, they can only be used for particular projects designated by the donor (and are, thus, linked to the donor's priorities and sometimes come with naming rights). They can rarely be used for operating expenses. For an example of the difficulties of transforming an endowment to reserves (in order to pay debt), see: Josh Moody, "Webster Seeks to Unrestrict Endowment Funds," *Inside Higher Ed*, February 24, 2024, https://www.insidehighered.com.

WHAT WAS ACHIEVED AT SALEM STATE, DESPITE THE OBSTACLES

A number of important achievements related to campus debt were attained by organizing at Salem State. Perhaps most significantly, we changed the conversation about the public funding of public higher education and helped reframe the common sense on this issue locally, statewide, and even nationally. Such dialogues now include campus debt and its consequences.[28] Certainly, the dialogue still includes false narratives about inevitably declining enrollment, an increased focus on professional/job training, the reduction of unnecessary and/or "inefficient" programs and departments (generally, but not exclusively, in the humanities and social sciences), and "excessive" salaries for union workers (but virtually nothing about administrative bloat).

At Salem State, the president of the local chapter, who was unaware of campus debt, has increasingly adopted it into her framework. The debt analysis has affected strategic planning, accreditation, and other university-wide processes. The debt reveal's analysis of campus expenditures and debts catalyzed the closing of an expensive and unnecessary off-campus office for the university president. This initiative also helped reduce the

---

[28] Massachusetts State College Association (MSCA)/Salem State Chapter, "Growth Plan for a Sustainable Salem State University," December 15, 2020.

furloughs from five to two weeks. Our organizing was scaled throughout Massachusetts, and we helped develop and share the debt reveal model nationally through PHEW and the Coalition against Campus Debt.

CHAPTER FOUR
GETTING STARTED:
REVEALING DEBT, PLANTING
SEEDS, AND BUILDING POWER

This chapter reviews the early power-building stages of debt-centered higher education organizing at the City University of New York (CUNY) and West Chester University of Pennsylvania (WCU). The debt stories from these institutions illustrate the highly classed and racialized foundations of public higher education debt financing in the twenty-first century. We also demonstrate how debt undergirded specific catalyzing issues on each campus: CUNY's pandemic-era cuts and layoffs and WCU's 2022 student housing crisis. While our coalition was personally connected to these two cases, they mirror the situation on hundreds of public campuses across the United States. We conclude by reflecting on the campus organizers' key strategies to initiate fights against the modern debt apparatus governing public higher education.

THE STORY OF HIGHER EDUCATION DEBT (IN TWO PARTS)

CUNY: A FALLEN PROMISE

The City University of New York (CUNY) spans twenty-five campuses across the city's five boroughs. It serves 243,000 undergraduate and graduate students. CUNY is the nation's largest public urban university and has a diverse student body—21 percent white, 31 percent Hispanic, 26 percent Black, and 22 percent Asian/Pacific Islander.[1] The CUNY student body is also largely working class—a full 50 percent of CUNY students report an annual household income under $30,000, and an even larger group are eligible for federal Pell Grants. This context is important for understanding CUNY's history as a singular example of possibility in the US public higher education landscape.

CUNY's origins are found in the City College of New York (CCNY), an all-male Free Academy established in 1847. In the following decades, CUNY added other institutions to provide city residents with high-quality, *tuition-free* postsecondary opportunities. In the post-WWII era, CUNY (along with the public systems in California and New York state) "would develop the largest and most comprehensive public university systems in

---

[1] CUNY, "About CUNY," *City University of New York*, n.d., https://www.cuny.edu.

the country."[2] In the years following the war, the City of New York spent $10.5 million annually to maintain free tuition at its four municipal colleges. This policy was respected like religious doctrine by the New York City Board of Higher Education (BHE).[3]

CUNY was an incredible commitment to social democracy but became increasingly selective under the pressures of student demand and limited space. Its population became more middle class, which impacted the already constrained racial and ethnic makeup of the system: "As late as 1967, CUNY's census revealed that 82 percent of its students were white, 10 percent black, and 3 percent Puerto Rican."[4] For context, 40 percent of the high school population was Black or Puerto Rican.[5]

In 1966, BHE institutionalized an open admission policy to ensure any New York City high school graduate could be admitted into CUNY. The plan was set to be implemented by 1975, but this was far too late for Black and Puerto Rican students who had already waited a decade for access. In February 1969, student organizers created the Black and Puerto Rican Student Community

---

[2] Michael Fabricant and Stephen Brier, *Austerity Blues: Fighting for the Soul of Public Higher Education* (Baltimore: Johns Hopkins University Press, 2016), 48.

[3] Fabricant and Brier, *Austerity Blues*, 51, 53.

[4] Fabricant and Brier, *Austerity Blues*, 67.

[5] Unknown, "Five Demands," *CUNY Digital History Archive*, May 1969, https://cdha.cuny.edu.

(BPRSC) and demanded that a policy of proportionate racial admissions be adopted immediately. When this and other demands went unanswered, Black and Puerto Rican students (along with white allies) secured various entrances and occupied several buildings on the City College of New York (CCNY) campus. On other campuses, students staged sit-ins and rallies; local high school students even engaged in actions that closed several secondary schools.[6]

According to the student organizers, negotiations were initiated, and progress was made during the subsequent two-week occupation. However, the BHE, under political pressure to reopen the school, interrupted negotiations by serving injunctions against the student occupiers.[7] Violent clashes between students, and between students and police culminated in several fires being set in university buildings. "The next day the CUNY Board of Higher Education effectively reversed its previous position and declared a commitment to meeting the demands of the strikers, including a policy of Open Admissions."[8] While this was less targeted than racially proportionate admissions, the open admissions policy meant that large numbers of white working-class students would also benefit

---

[6] Christopher Gunderson, "The Struggle for CUNY A History of the CUNY Student Movement, 1969–1999" (PhD diss., CUNY, 2014).

[7] Gunderson, "The Struggle for CUNY."

[8] Gunderson, "The Struggle for CUNY," 8.

from the strike led by Black and Puerto Rican students.[9]

Before the 1969 strike, 78 percent of first-year students were white; "by 1975, that percentage was 30."[10] The open admissions policy had two important outcomes for CUNY's future: "The first was the creation of a base of white support for the new policy as white working-class youth who would never have gotten into CUNY under the old admissions standards were let in en masse. The second was to dramatically increase the costs and strains that the policy put on the university."[11]

CUNY's transition occurred alongside dramatic shifts in New York City's social and economic landscape. Jobs began to disappear as white and middle-class flight to the suburbs increased, deepening already-existing poverty. The city of "New York was spending more than it was earning in revenues."[12] Yet, the state prevented the city from levying higher taxes. Political leaders were faced with a tough choice: cut services or borrow the money. They decided to "mobilize financial mechanisms to displace the conflicts the city confronted in the present onto the future."[13] However, the

---

[9] Gunderson, "The Struggle for CUNY."

[10] Fabricant and Brier, *Austerity Blues*, 84.

[11] Gunderson, "The Struggle for CUNY," 8.

[12] Kimberly Phillips-Fein, *Fear City: New York's Fiscal Crisis and the Rise of Austerity Politics* (New York: Metropolitan Books, 2017).

[13] Phillips-Fein, *Fear City*.

borrowing terms were detrimental to the ideal of democratic governance in public institutions.

Shortly after opening its doors to a more diverse student population (racially and class), CUNY began charging students tuition. The New York governor, Nelson Rockefeller, had sought tuition charges for years to underwrite private bonds to fund university construction projects. However, BHE resisted until pushed to the brink of fiscal collapse in 1975. The city came under the control of the banking industry, as managed by the Emergency Financial Control Board (EFCB), and CUNY's budget was cut by tens of millions of dollars.[14] In exchange for a state takeover of the senior colleges' finances, tuition charges were enacted in the CUNY system. The imposition of tuition eroded the promise of accessible public higher education in New York City. By the end of the decade, "CUNY suffered a decline of sixty-two thousand students. . . with 50 percent fewer black and Latino freshmen among CUNY's entering class in 1980."[15]

The elimination of CUNY's free college tradition was part of a wider project of *disciplining through debt* spearheaded by conservative politicians to hamper the social democratic possibilities being demanded by university students in the sixties and seventies. Ronald Reagan, then California's governor, was one of the first to utilize a tuition policy to destroy "disruptive elements" on col-

---

[14] Fabricant and Brier, *Austerity Blues*.

[15] Fabricant and Brier, *Austerity Blues*, 88.

lege campuses.[16] Reagan's regime understood and sought to impede the radical future that could be fostered by a free and fully accessible university. As Reagan's advisor, Roger Freeman, stated in 1970, "We are in danger of producing an educated proletariat. That's dynamite! We have to be selective on who we allow to go through (higher education)."[17] Reagan relentlessly lobbied the California legislature to impose tuition and, in the years following his two terms as governor, the UC system would charge additional fees and tuition for the first time. In a debate on the policy, Reagan casually explained that the new tuition would "be accompanied by adequate loans to be paid back after graduation."[18] This disciplining of working-class students through debt would kickstart a national shift: from funding public higher education through tax dollars to privately financing public higher education through individual and institutional debt. As will be demonstrated in Chapter 6, this tactic has now been utilized against the working-class students, faculty, and staff of the University of Puerto Rico as well.

---

[16] Jon Schwarz, "The Origin of Student Debt: Reagan Adviser Warned Free College Would Create a Dangerous "Educated Proletariat," *The Intercept*, August 26, 2022, https://theintercept.com.

[17] Genevieve Carlton, "How the Threat of an 'Educated Proletariat' Created the Student Debt Crisis," *BestColleges*, September 8, 2022, https://www.bestcolleges.com.

[18] Ronald Reagan, "January 17, 1967 Statement of Governor Ronald Reagan on Tuition," *Ronald Reagan Presidential Library and Museum*, n.d., https://www.reaganlibrary.gov.

In the decades since CUNY imposed tuition, "the ratio of tuition paid by full-time students to public funding has shifted from zero to about 50 percent."[19] This necessitates increased reliance on student loans to fund postsecondary education, particularly for working-class and students of color. CUNY has experienced a distinct shift from a tax-financed system to a debt-financed system, and student lending is not the only debt mechanism at play. Between 2008 and 2021, CUNY saw a 60 percent increase in total long-term debt (totaling $5.6 billion). Institutional debt is now also at the heart of the system's story.

WEST CHESTER UNIVERSITY: THE NEGLECT OF THE STATE

West Chester University (WCU)—originally a state-supported normal school to prepare teachers—joined thirteen other institutions to found the Pennsylvania State System of Higher Education (PASSHE) in 1983. WCU is currently the largest institution in PASSHE, with 17,552 undergraduate and graduate students in 2021. WCU is much less racially diverse than CUNY: the student body is 73 percent white, 7 percent Hispanic/Latino, 12 percent Black, and 3 percent Asian/Pacific Islander. Likewise, only 24 percent of students receive Pell Grants.

PASSHE's founding legislation states that the system's purpose "shall be to provide high qual-

---

[19] Fabricant and Brier, *Austerity Blues*, 3.

ity education *at the lowest possible cost to students*" (emphasis added). Therefore, unlike CUNY, it never had ambitions for free tuition. West Chester University has applied tuition and other charges from its founding (though the institution routinely offered private scholarship opportunities to needy undergraduate students). Individualized debt financing through student loans was also present in WCU's early history. The first Alumni Loan Fund appeared in the undergraduate catalog as far back as 1905 and served the explicit purpose of providing interest-free loans "to worthy students preparing to teach."[20] Even with the introduction of state funding in the early twentieth century, the undergraduate catalog (in 1937) continued to promote additional student loan funds and employment opportunities to aid students in "securing an education." This suggests that students have long struggled to finance their studies at WCU.

WCU (and PASSHE) experienced a dramatic shift in funding during the neoliberal era. In 1983, when the state system was founded, student tuition and fees covered approximately 37 percent of expenses at PASSHE schools.[21] By 2020, nearly 72 percent of education costs at four-year public

[20] West Chester University, "WCU Digital Collections – Undergraduate Catalogues," *West Chester University Library*, n.d., https://library.wcupa.edu.

[21] Diana Polson, Stephen Herzenberg, and Mark Price, "At Students' Expense: Rising Costs Threaten Pennsylvania Public Universities' Role in Upward Mobility," *Keystone Research Center*, June 8, 2017, https://keystoneresearch.org.

institutions in Pennsylvania were paid by students.[22] This transition from a majority tax-funded system to a majority student- (and student debt-) funded system was accelerated during Governor Tom Corbett's administration. Corbett—part of the Tea Party wave of 2010—secured the governorship with an outspoken agenda to create friendlier conditions for natural gas drilling and to privatize the PreK–12 education system with a statewide voucher program. Despite struggling to secure these policy changes in the legislature, he united conservatives around a project of fiscal austerity after the Great Recession. This austerity hit hardest in the state's public school systems. The Corbett administration infamously oversaw a $1 billion reduction in PreK–12 spending, which "rippled across the state in the form of teacher layoffs, program cancellations, and local property tax increases."[23] Due to Pennsylvania's pre-existing inequitable funding formula, these cuts were highly discriminatory; students of color faced twice the funding cuts ($728 per student) as the average white student ($366 per student).[24]

---

[22] PASSHE, "FY 2022–23 Appropriations Request Summary," *Pennsylvania State System of Higher Education*, n.d., https://www.passhe.edu.

[23] Thomas Fitzgerald and Angela Couloumbis, "'A Thousand Cuts' and One Big One: How Corbett's Fate Was Sealed," *The Philadelphia Inquirer*, November 5, 2014, https://www.inquirer.com.

[24] Public Interest Law Center, "New Study Shows State Cuts to Education Highly Discriminatory," *The Public Interest Law Center*, n.d., https://pubintlaw.org.

The State System of Higher Education was not spared in this post-recession hack job; Corbett cut the PASSHE budget by $31 million (nearly 20 percent). This led to dramatic reductions in faculty, classes, and programs, as well as a 7.5 percent tuition increase in 2011-2012.[25] Tuition increases (between 2.5 and 3.5 percent) were administered for each of the following six years, covering a frozen state budget. This ongoing austerity pushed debt burdens onto students and the PASSHE institutions themselves. In the decade after the Corbett cuts, institutional debt increased by almost 30 percent at PASSHE's schools. At WCU, this resulted in a more than 140 percent increase in debt service.

During this time, WCU—quickly becoming the largest institution in the system—began to pursue independence from PASSHE. A 2014 PA State Senate Bill was introduced to allow schools to secede from the state system and become 'state-related' (e.g., Temple University, Penn State University, and the University of Pittsburgh). Such schools receive a limited amount of state funding in exchange for providing tuition discounts to in-state students. The state-related universities are private entities that own their assets independently of the Commonwealth, so there is no governmental check on tuition and fees. Students at state-related

---

[25] Steve Hicks, "The Miseducation of Mr. Corbett: APSCUF President Offers Facts on Public Higher Education in Pennsylvania," *Association of Pennsylvania State College & University Faculties*, February 17, 2012, https://www.apscuf.org.

schools pay significantly more than those attending publicly owned schools.

The succession bill was sponsored by Andy Dinniman (a former WCU faculty member) and Tommy Tomlinson (a WCU trustee). They worked with the institution's private fundraising arm, West Chester University Foundation, to campaign for the bill. The council of trustees even requested that the Foundation hire the Bravo Group, a Harrisburg lobbying and public relations firm, to campaign for the bill's passage.[26] These powerful players worked to convince stakeholders that privatizing WCU was in the best interest of students. However, major criticisms were also levied against the bill. Public education advocates maintained that the secession of the largest PASSHE institution would destroy public higher education in the Commonwealth and deprive smaller institutions of essential funding streams. Opponents also noted that secession would require WCU to purchase all the publicly held lands and buildings on campus from PASSHE, thereby placing the institution in significant debt. These millions of dollars in debt owed to the state could only be serviced with two potential revenue sources: unrestricted assets or student tuition. Fortunately, the bill failed.

However, WCU had been quietly (even covertly) taking steps to ease the succession process. Colleen

---

[26] Bill Schackner, "West Chester University's Foundation Bankrolling Effort to Exit State System," *Pittsburgh Post-Gazette*, March 15, 2014, https://www.post-gazette.com.

Bradley, the former WCU director of budget and financial planning and a whistleblower, revealed that the WCU administration pressured her to report millions in budget deficits when the institution was actually running a surplus. Bradley alleges that WCU "claimed break-even or deficit budgets" while increasing its holdings by $56.6 million over three years,[27] all to substantially increase its unrestricted net assets and position itself to secede from PASSHE. Another move that seemed to prepare for secession was the formation of a private dormitory subsidiary, University Student Housing (USH). It built expensive dorms to meet WCU's increasing enrollment demands. While more publicly owned, subsidized dorms would have added to WCU's potential tab should it secede from the state system, private dormitories (owned and operated by the Foundation) would easily and painlessly transfer. The debt incurred from these buildings would not appear on WCU's books. Instead, USH was listed as the borrower. Nevertheless, the WCU administration was still 'on the hook' for these loans

"In 2013, the university penned a cooperation agreement with USH that, among other things, stipulated that WCU would 'limit the use and growth' of the public dorms."[28] This agreement

[27] Susan Snyder, "West Chester U. Seeks Dismissal of Whistle-Blower Suit," *The Philadelphia Inquirer*, July 21, 2015, https://www.inquirer.com.

[28] David Backer, "Planned Scarcity in Public University Housing," *Schooling in Socialist America*, December 19, 2022, https://buttondown.email.

barred the university from constructing, owning, or operating any additional new on- or off-campus housing and bound it to "take off-line or demolish" nearly 400 existing public beds. This "planned scarcity"[29] would make the USH dormitories the primary residence option for WCU students over the coming decade. The debt USH incurred from their building would be passed directly onto students via housing costs that were nearly three times higher than the public dorms. For hundreds of WCU students, the cost of living on campus could be thousands of dollars more than the cost of tuition—a fact that pushed the average debt burdens of WCU graduates to over $37,000.[30]

CAMPUS CRISES AND BUILDING POWER

The story of public higher education in the United States is a debt story, so it is also a story of crises. In the neoliberal era, public institutions like CUNY and WCU are frequently rocked with fiscal crises, emergencies, and "unprecedented times." Whether real or exaggerated, administrators make claims on institutional resources that dramatically impact the student experience and the working conditions of faculty and staff. Course and program cuts, layoffs and furloughs, privatization, and outsourcing all come to pass when fiscal "emergencies" hit indebted

[29] Backer, "Planned Scarcity."

[30] TICAS, "Student Debt for College Graduates in Pennsylvania," *The Institute for College Access & Success*, 2020, https://ticas.org.

public institutions. These moments of austerity and labor extraction have serious consequences for those who study and work on campus. However, they also present important opportunities to organize against debt financing in higher education. Nowhere else are so many debtors (public institutions included) concentrated together and debts are never more salient than in moments of crisis.

This section considers two debt crises at CUNY and WCU. We examine the CUNY system's cuts at the height of the COVID-19 pandemic and WCU's post-pandemic housing crisis. We also detail the early steps of debt organizing that were spurred by these issues, including CUNY organizers' participation in the National Debt Reveal and WCU student organizers' work on campus housing debt. Each group of organizers increased the success of their work by 1) centering an organizing theory of change, 2) engaging in concerted political education, and 3) taking advantage of existing infrastructure to organize.

THE NATIONAL DEBT REVEAL

In the spring of 2020, faculty and staff from across the US came together to create the Public Higher Education Workers (PHEW) Network. While these higher education workers and unionists had been meeting monthly for some time, the group only solidified during the pandemic to provide vision and strategies for a burgeoning postsecondary labor movement. PHEW began hosting webinars about how workers could organize to protect their colleges and universities from the onslaught of austerity and protect themselves and their students from hazardous working and learning conditions. However, these important conversations routinely encountered a seemingly insurmountable roadblock: institutional debt. Organizers consistently observed their managers answering to powerful, unseen forces that did not mind throwing workers—or even the basic purpose of the institutions (i.e., teaching and learning)—under the bus. Debt was a structural barrier to creating colleges and universities that truly served the public.

A small PHEW working group (including many of the authors) started to investigate the prevalence of debt at their institutions. We began hosting additional webinars and created a debt research toolkit to teach others how to investigate the impact of institutional debt on their campuses. All of this organizing culminated in the National Debt Reveal Day on April 15th, 2021.[31] We convened with workers from dozens of institutions who took to social media to reveal the debt totals of their schools, as well as the concrete consequences of servicing such debt. The organizers used the Debt Reveal Toolkit to ask and answer questions like: How many additional faculty positions or class sections could my school have without institutional debt? How much less would the average student

---

[31] Eleni Shirmer, Jason Thomas Wozniak, Dana Morrison, Rich Levy, and Joanna Gonsalves, "American Universities Are Buried Under a Mountain of Debt," *The Nation*, April 15, 2021, https://www.thenation.com.

loan bill be at my school without institutional debt? How is my school beholden to powerful creditors?

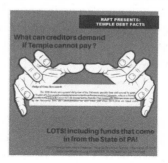

Social media posts from the National Debt Reveal Day.

This organizing was aided by the concerted dissemination of the Debt Reveal Toolkit, which contained a preconstructed worksheet to guide local research on the ground. Workers only needed a few key public documents from their institutions to complete the worksheet and calculate the true human cost of their school's debt. These costs—what we termed *instructional harm* measures—were powerful pieces of evidence that could be disseminated through political education and local campaign demands. To date, hundreds of higher education workers—faculty, students, and staff—have been provided with the Debt Reveal Toolkit.

THE CUNY COVID-19 CRISIS

In the spring of 2020, New York City was rocked by one of the most horrific waves of COVID-19 deaths in the world. By mid-April, deaths averaged more than 750 per day and the city ground to a halt. The CUNY community was particularly impacted by what is believed to be the highest death toll of any higher education system in the country.[32] CUNY students and their families—largely working-class New Yorkers whose jobs provided essential front-line services—were among those hardest hit.

Just as communities began to emerge from the weight of such trauma, the CUNY system announced it would be laying off 2,800 part-time adjunct faculty and staff. These cuts—more than twenty percent of all adjunct positions—impacted student services, course offerings, and degree completion. At the same time, hundreds more adjunct CUNY workers lost access to health insurance due to reduced workloads. The Professional Staff

---

[32] CUNY, "CUNY Hosts University-wide Day of Remembrance," City University of New York, May 17, 2022, https://www1.cuny.edu.

Congress (PSC), the union representing 30,000 CUNY faculty and staff, immediately filed a lawsuit arguing that the layoffs violated the premise of the Coronavirus Aid, Relief and Economic Security (CARES) Act, which provided financial support to stabilize institutional payrolls and prevent cuts.

The lawsuit ultimately failed, leaving the workers in a state of limbo and without access to medical care during a global pandemic. Many PSC members who were critical of the union's reliance on legalistic methods, as opposed to collective power, began petitioning for a strike authorization vote to protect the most vulnerable workers. In particular, a militant group of CUNY unionists, Rank and File Action (RAFA), led the charge for alternatives to shock doctrine austerity. RAFA organizers in the PHEW network joined the institutional debt working group, intent on revealing how CUNY's debt contributed to such cruel neoliberal crises.

Soon, other union members began to attend the PHEW-hosted debt workshops to theorize, identify, and make real the impact of their institution's debt. RAFA and PSC members uncovered the instructional harms of debt and began organizing local CUNY debt reveal events to encourage more stakeholders to call for an end to debt-driven austerity policies. The organizers engaged in a months-long effort to 1) raise awareness of the issue of institutional debt and 2) turn people out to these events. As CUNY organizer Zoe Hu recounted, these existing networks "provided a really convenient infrastructure for getting people

involved and spreading awareness." At the height of
the pandemic, in the absence of face-to-face workplace conversations, PSC and RAFA's tools helped
the organizers reach the organizable.

The first reveal event hosted by CUNY organizers was a Zoom teach-in on the impact of CUNY
debt. Organizers highlighted the reality of debt in
the CUNY budget, the undemocratic prioritization
of creditors over the public good, and the racialized
austerity practices that had been implemented as
a result. This teach-in carefully revealed how debt
mechanisms not only guided long-term funding
deficits, but also played a role in the orchestrated
pandemic layoffs. More importantly, this event
provided space for CUNY organizers to delegitimize the debt regime. They provided workers and
students with the language to challenge ubiqui-
tous financial practices in neoliberal public higher
education.

CUNY organizers also hosted an in-person
rally in Brooklyn in conjunction with the teach-
in. Workers and students spoke out about the
impacts of CUNY's cuts on their lives. With more
than thirty people in attendance, participants
shared personal accounts of their experiences with
debt-driven austerity policies to show the human
consequences of cuts. Each of the CUNY events
also ended with a clear set of demands that imag-
ined what an institutional budget for *the people*
might look like. Of course, organizers demanded
cancelling all CUNY debt; this was then followed
by demands for a liberatory budget that would

move funding away from upper administration, police, and surveillance, and toward free tuition, smaller class sizes, health care, childcare, access to safe housing, a diverse faculty workforce, and worker protections.

This analysis of higher education austerity at CUNY supported workers in pushing back against narratives (from administrators and even union leadership) that institutional debt was a necessary standard practice. The debt reveal work destabilized this narrative by first surfacing these assumptions and then making the familiar strange. The debt reveal also encouraged workers to see organizing as an essential part of a collective theory of change. However, this early work also led to many organizing reflections. Next steps were difficult under the overwhelming assault of neoliberal austerity and with so many organizers in precarious positions and working long hours. Many higher education workers—especially adjunct and graduate workers—are pulled in many directions, hindering their ability to make inroads within the larger system. At CUNY, organizers were also forced to respond to racist attacks on campuses, cuts to programs, hiring freezes, and increased workloads, which slowed their initial debt organizing.

THE WCU STUDENT HOUSING CRISIS

On December 9, 2022, in the midst of fall semester finals, 825 students received letters from the WCU administration revoking their university housing for the following year. The planned scarcity of privatized student housing had finally reached its breaking point. That same semester, the institution enrolled the largest freshman class in its 150-year history.[33] Increasing numbers of students applied for the institution's more affordable public dormitories (given the rising numbers of out-of-state students and high prices for off-campus apartments). Rejected students were told to either obtain a costly off-campus apartment or join the waitlist for the expensive private USH dorms. Instead, they immediately began organizing a rally and march.

Members of Students for Socialism and Liberation (SFS) were key to this initial organizing. Many SFS organizers cut their teeth two summers before fighting PASSHE university consolidations with the statewide student-led group *PASSHE Defenders.* SFS was prepared to spring into action and organize a rally for WCU students mere days after the letters went out. They created a social media presence with the handle @WCUHousingCrisis and began outreach to impacted students and media outlets. Just three days after students were denied affordable housing, more than fifty students congregated in front of the president's office to share their stories and how the decision would impact their lives. In the typical quiet of finals week, local news outlets documented

---

[33] Holly Herman, "West Chester University Enrolls Largest Freshman Class," *West Chester, PA Patch*, October 13, 2022, https://patch.com.

dozens of students shouting, "housing is a human right" from all corners of the campus.

Over the extended winter break, SFS organizers began holding meetings with members and impacted students to document and study the crisis. They drew on research by WCU faculty organizers, who had been studying the university's neoliberal student housing history. This research identified: 1) the complicated public-private relationship between WCU, the Foundation, and USH; 2) the millions of dollars of debt the private entity acquired to finance buildings; and 3) the egregious cooperation agreement that took public dorms offline.

This political education ultimately informed the group's demands for immediate housing stipends for impacted students, the development of new *public* dorms, and the reversal of USH's private housing facilities into more affordable, university-owned dorms. The student demands continued over winter break as they sought to raise consciousness amongst students, faculty, staff, and community stakeholders through concerted political education. The students created infographics that detailed the egregious history of WCU's housing privatization, drafted an open letter to the student newspaper, and supported members in writing blog posts about the crisis. This work was all public facing and intended to bring more students, staff, and faculty into the movement.

In the first weeks of the next semester, university president Christopher Fiorentino offered a direct response. Fiorentino granted one-time scholarships to impacted students that would cover $2,000 in housing costs. He also "[broke with] historic practices implemented by previous University and State System administrations" by announcing a cabinet-level decision that all future housing would be university-owned, public dormitories. However, Fiorentino denied the students' expropriative demand that private USH dorms be converted into affordable public dorms. He argued that one powerful barrier prevented this: *debt*. The university could not pursue expropriation of the private dorms due to the cost of transferring USH debt to WCU, which the president estimated would be $200 million. Fiorentino stated that "Those costs would have to be passed on to students through increased housing fees," making it a nonstarter.

Engaged faculty and student organizers immediately began developing responses. They argued that the university should not be "on the hook" for paying the estimated $200 million to purchase the USH debt; rather, the Commonwealth of Pennsylvania should foot the bill. Organizers contended that it was the state's responsibility to pay for the infrastructure of public institutions (i.e., dorms), especially when there was a $5.4 billion budget surplus in the capital. After all, the only reason the debt existed in the first place was because the Commonwealth historically shirked its responsibility.

The student organizers soon ran into internal conflicts and structural barriers (much like the

CUNY organizers). However, the statewide faculty union—the Association of Pennsylvania State College and University Faculties (APSCUF)—began lobbying efforts around this institutional debt narrative. As APSCUF president Ken Mash wrote in a monthly faculty newsletter:

> WE ARE STATE-OWNED UNIVERSITIES. . . . We are not organized as private or state-related universities. We do not have tremendous foundations. We are owned and operated by the Commonwealth. Ultimately, it is not university debt: it is Pennsylvania's debt. It is absurd enough that private funds have to be used for something that is ultimately the asset of the state, but the absurdity rises to incredible heights when one starts to think about how current students have to bear the burden of that debt. They are denied the faculty, the programs, the options, the support, and other services they might otherwise get because they must contribute to the servicing of that debt.

Shortly thereafter, faculty at some of the most financially vulnerable institutions in the state system began investigating institutional debt with members of our debt working group. After a few meetings, they collected the information needed to lobby state politicians. Within a couple of months, these schools were granted a $65 million line item in the 2023–2024 budget that would go directly toward paying their longstanding legacy debt burden.

The increasing identification of institutional debt in PASSHE indicates a clear shift in how faculty, students, staff, and the wider community view public higher education financing. While this shift was important, it only obtained partial successes without concerted and sustained grassroots organizing. After all, PASSHE retains over $1.9 billion in debt, with some schools disproportionately impacted by the weight of annual debt service. Like with the CUNY debt reveal, the efforts at WCU raised consciousness but fell short of a wider campaign for relieving public universities of debt financing that negatively impacts faculty, staff, students, and their institutions.

ORGANIZING ANALYSIS

These examples of early debt organizing at CUNY and WCU illustrate how to begin localized organizing against university debt financing. Each case reveals the importance of grounding efforts in an organizing theory of change that centers political education and the use of existing organizational infrastructure to build power amongst a growing base of institutional stakeholders. Workers and students at CUNY and WCU envisioned change as a project of mass participation and collective action in their public-facing efforts to construct a movement and demand a true university of the people.

POLITICAL EDUCATION

Concerted political education was key in planting the seeds of a collective movement. An organizing approach should activate "people's sense of agency within the relations that compel participation yet deny equal power."[34] The organizers' political education efforts—local learning meetings, debt workshops, teach-ins, social media content, and op-eds—all helped activate agency. This type of political education is a necessary prerequisite for engaging everyday people in a movement against institutional debt financing. After all, it is impossible to fight something that you don't know exists. Debtor-creditor power relations are buried in institutional budgets, loan documents, debt covenants, and cooperation agreements. Higher education workers and students have commonly missed this target when pushing back against austerity.

Political education efforts must historicize and delegitimize the contemporary debt state, which has become accepted as standard practice in the neoliberal era. The organizers at these two schools named the existence of institutional debt *and* linked it to failures to deliver on the promise of public higher education. Such political education reframes the present reality of austerity and debt, not as an inevitability (as most administrators argue), but as a political decision that can be unmade just as easily as it was made.

---

[34] Shirmer et al., "American Universities."

Lastly, their political education efforts interspersed the language of critique with what Henry Giroux calls the *language of possibility*. The organizers put forth a vision of what the university could be in their careful construction and dissemination of radical, liberatory demands. At CUNY, organizers not only called for debt cancellation but also promoted an in-depth 'people's budget' as an explicit foil to the debt-driven austerity crisis. At WCU, the students demanded an expropriation of the private debt-controlled dorms, highlighting the ethical essentiality of guaranteeing public housing to public university students. Thus, political education served the critical function of defining the horizon toward which a growing collective can move.

ORGANIZATIONAL INFRASTRUCTURE

CUNY and WCU organizers also strategically identified and utilized existing organizational infrastructure to bring people into their educational activities and grow their base. They did not reinvent the wheel (in the pandemic, nonetheless) but built on pre-existing relationships. At CUNY, organizers recognized the importance of the PSC union and RAFA activist collective. The CUNY organizers used listservs, social media accounts, message groups, and even personal contacts to expand their reach and build solidarity with increasingly larger groups of workers and students. Their debt reveal work even brought in faculty from the Member

Action Coalition (MAC) of SUNY's faculty union, who took the issue of public higher education financing statewide.

At WCU, organizers from the SFS drew on their existing university relationships with students, faculty, staff, and other organizations to increase participation in their public actions and social media education campaigns. SFS was already considered a watchdog of PASSHE institutional governance after building positive organizing relationships fighting against PASSHE university consolidations. The SFS community used @StudentHousingCrisis political education—social media, local learning meetings, rallies, and publications—to grow their base and push back *against* the housing letters and *for* their demands.

Both CUNY and WCU highlight the importance of utilizing existing infrastructure for broader coalition-building in the earliest stages of institutional debt organizing. These cases, while only at the beginning of their journeys, provide organizers with meaningful insights and strategies for taking the first steps toward organizing on their campuses.

LESSONS LEARNED

Each case also generated important organizing lessons and reflections. The lackluster commitment from the major campus unions was particularly disappointing. We believe that public education workers hold a critical position in the fight for justice and the commons. Yet, this can only be realized when workers, *their unions*, and the broader community join in the fight for democratic teaching and learning spaces. The work of amassing power through grassroots coalition building is the most important task of unions and academic worker organizations in the neoliberal era. However, faculty and staff unions often see such efforts as distractions from the 'real' work of rhetorically persuading managers and politicians not to cut too deep. Inspired by abolitionist Frederick Douglass, we understand that power concedes nothing without a demand. Decades of status quo "business unionism" have proven this true as public higher education workers have steadily lost ground, year in and year out.

The importance of a fighting, democratic union in successful campus debt organizing cannot be overstated. The day-to-day work of coalition building is painstaking, and faculty, students, and staff at public institutions are already spread thin. Student organizers leading fights against cuts impacting the entire community often attend class and work full-time. Similarly, many adjunct and staff organizers are underpaid, overworked, and have precarious job security. Worker unions must step in to financially support and, in many cases, take on the work of organizing a coalition against institutional debt. Only when campus unions are reformed into member-driven, militant labor organizations will we be able to fully recognize the possibility of winning the institutions we all deserve.

CHAPTER FIVE
SCALING UP DEBT
ORGANIZING EFFORTS

This chapter highlights organizing work undertaken in 2022 to scale up legislative pressure and break the cycle of debt in the Massachusetts public higher education system. We fought to free students from the bonds of student debt and to free public universities from the debt obligations governing them. This case study offers strategies and practices for state-level organizing and coalition building that may be useful for other worker-led campaigns against debt financing.

The authors of this book struggled with next steps after the 2021 National Debt Reveal. What exactly should the debt reveals accomplish beyond exposing the problem and making demands to campus administrators? We knew worker and student debt revealing was a helpful tool for building power and achieving local campus and/or union goals. Revealing debt and its harmful effects fueled organizing against relentless, debt-imposed austerity. For instance, the Salem State University debt reveal pushed Massachusetts State College Association (MSCA) members to stand out against furloughs and the management's downsizing plans.[1] The union's rallying call became "protect people not buildings!"

We wondered whether debt revealing could morph into a broader movement to end the privatization of public education and work for reparatory justice. Could we draw up demands for the full cancellation of capital debt on all public campuses and/or the full cancellation of student debt (given that a huge portion of student debt services campus debt)? Such a project to end capitalistic schemes that undermine public education as a public good and put millions of students in debt would certainly require national organizing. Our coalition did not have the capacity for this type of growth, but we did have strong roots in progressive labor organizations. We chose not to draft a debt abolition manifesto but to keep the momentum through ongoing revealing. Our next step was to scale up campus debt organizing with a pilot campaign. Specifically, we aimed to move from individual campus struggles to an entire state system in our utopian goal of free, liberatory institutions of higher learning governed by their members. We assessed the public university systems where we already had some traction: Colorado, Massachusetts, Pennsylvania, and New York.

In the fall of 2021, we selected Massachusetts as the pilot project site. Three authors—Barbara, Rich, and Joanna—already had deep connec-

---

[1] Rich Levy and Joanna Gonsalves, "Our Faculty Union Exposed the University's Debt—and Who's Paying for It," *Labor Notes*, August 26, 2023, https://labornotes.org.

tions with the statewide Massachusetts Teachers Association (MTA) and its higher education locals. Furthermore, Educators for a Democratic Union (EDU), a progressive caucus in the MTA, had pushed the union to adopt democratic processes for more than a decade. In response, the MTA leadership created structures (staff positions, committees, and grants) to support member-driven organizing around worker respect and pay equity, racial and social justice, and reclaiming education as a critical public good. Joanna and Rich tapped into MTA resources to launch a statewide debt reveal for all the public universities in Massachusetts.

UNDERSTANDING HOW MASSACHUSETTS PUBLIC UNIVERSITIES GOT DEEP INTO DEBT

The Massachusetts debt reveal project first dove into the history of capital funding in the state's public higher education system. This research clarified what needed to be changed and confirmed that campus and state leaders were not going to do this work. Given the bipartisan appeal of the neoliberal paradigm, very few elected and appointed officials are committed to truly improving public higher education—even fewer are willing to propose reparative plans. We found that the Commonwealth had created campus debt traps that subjected generations of students to increasing indebtedness and ensured a perpetual, antidemocratic state of austerity on public campuses. The Massachusetts debt story—compiled from scores of state documents—

was shared with our workers, students, alumni, administrators, and elected officials as an organizing strategy to push for legislative change.

Public universities in Massachusetts began as three colleges (so-called "normal schools") that were established in 1839 and 1840 to provide free liberal arts education to mostly white aspiring educators (these original institutions have become Framingham State, Westfield State, and Bridgewater State).[2] By the turn of the century, there were seven more state normal schools and a public agricultural college (now UMass Amherst). These were built with state dollars, federal Morrill funds, and on land stolen from Indigenous people.[3] After World War II, community colleges were established, and the normal school campuses were transformed into comprehensive state colleges to address workforce needs and accommodate the surge of (white male veteran) students taking advantage of newly estab-

---

[2] Mary-Lou Breitborde and Kelly Kolodney, "Remembering Massachusetts State Normal Schools: Pioneers in Teacher Education," *Historical Journal of Massachusetts* 43, no. 1 (Winter 2015): 22–39.

[3] The 1862 Morrill Land Grant College Act established a grant program for states to build colleges to "benefit the agricultural and mechanical arts." Act of July 2, 1862 (Morrill Act), Public Law 37-108, 12 STAT 503, which established land grant colleges; 7/2/1862; Enrolled Acts and Resolutions of Congress, 1789–2011; General Records of the United States Government, Record Group 11; National Archives Building, Washington, DC, https://www.archives.gov/milestone-documents/morrill-act. See also Robert Lee and Tristan Ahtone, "Stolen Indigenous land is the foundation of the land-grant university system. Climate change is its legacy," *High Country News*," March 30, 2020, https://www.hcn.org.

lished federal grants. The Commonwealth paid for the construction of these public campuses, passing few, if any, of the construction costs onto the students. Commonwealth audits from 1920 to 1940 reveal routine annual appropriations for campus construction and repairs, including dormitories and dining halls.[4]

The long, steady decline in the Commonwealth's support for public higher education began in the mid-sixties, once it was no longer used to fund the full cost of higher education. New laws declared that Commonwealth dollars could no longer fund the construction and renovation of "auxiliary buildings" that accommodated the growing residential student population.[5] Instead, the Massachusetts state legislature established two authorities to finance campus capital projects through revenue bonds: the University of Massachusetts Building Authority (UMBA) and the Massachusetts State College Building Authority (MSCBA). The individual public campuses backed their loans with projected student revenue from fees charged for housing, dining, parking, and recreation. While borrowing was initially minimal, the idea that students, not the

---

[4] Massachusetts State Archives, *Report of the Auditor of the Commonwealth of Massachusetts for the Fiscal Year Ending 1920* (Boston: Wright & Potter, Printing Co, 1921), 31–2.

[5] Michael N. Bastedo, "Thwarted Ambition: The Role of Public Policy in University Development," *New England Journal of Public Policy* 20, no. 2 (2005): 45–65.

Commonwealth, were responsible for the capital costs of auxiliary services had taken hold.[6]

By the nineties, Massachusetts public colleges had accumulated several billion dollars in deferred maintenance after three decades of underfunding. Thus, the UMBA and MSCBA were given control over the *repairs* of existing auxiliary buildings and forced campuses to borrow for these expenses too.[7] This move shifted millions of dollars in annual capital maintenance costs away from the Commonwealth and onto student fees.

UMBA has accumulated a staggering $3.7 billion in capital assets across the UMass campuses; the MSCBA owns forty-two residential complexes and other facilities.[8] Because the buildings sit on land owned by the Commonwealth, universities cannot use these buildings as collateral for their loans, so they must back loans with student fees. Following suit, the building authorities were allowed to set the student fees and create debt-service reserve accounts with the fees to establish

---

[6] This differentially impacts the college success of white middle-class students compared with low-income students and students of color; Marcella Bombardieri, "Massachusetts excels at higher education -for the white and well-off," *Boston Globe*, January 28, 2020, https://www.bostonglobe.com.

[7] University of Massachusetts Building Authority, *History of the UMBA on the Occasion of its 50th Anniversary* (Shrewbury, MA: UMBA, 2010).

[8] UMBA, "Financial Statements and Auditors Report, Fiscal Year 2022," *University of Massachusetts Building Authority*, n.d., https://www.umassba.org; MSCBA, "Capital Projects Report, 2016," *Massachusetts State College Building Authority*, n.d., https://www.mscba.org.

bond-worthiness. Initially, the Commonwealth pledged to cover debt service if student fee revenue and debt reserves were insufficient to cover debt payments. However, this guarantee was taken away as the state government continued down a privatization path, putting public colleges and universities in a more precarious position. If student revenues and reserves from auxiliary services dry up (e.g., due to lower occupancy in the dorms or the unexpected closure of a campus facility), state appropriations for educational operations (which is mostly campus employee payroll) can be intercepted to pay outstanding debt service.[9] In effect, the Commonwealth has completely shirked its financial responsibility to any and all auxiliary building debt.

Debt financing is now the norm under relentless state-imposed austerity. Today, the state government even expects campuses to pay for a significant portion of *academic* building construction.[10] For example,

---

[9] Massachusetts Legislature, "General Law, Acts of 1998, Chapter 290," *Massachusetts Legislature*, August 10, 1998, https://malegislature.gov.

[10] We can only point to one moment in the last fifty years where the Commonwealth took some responsibility for campus infrastructure. In 2008, with a strong economy (just prior to the Great Recession), Governor Deval Patrick recognized that public colleges are critical for "the Commonwealth's future, and in the future of our students" and signed off on a $2.2 billion bond bill for construction projects on every one of the twenty-nine state campuses. A review of public records showed that the state's commitment to these projects approached 100 percent of the total construction costs. This support for campus infrastructure was a short-lived bright spot for Massachusetts public higher education, but still did not fully address the

in 2022, Governor Charlie Baker announced support for STEM facilities on four campuses but only provided about 50 percent of the project funding.[11] Salem State was awarded funding for Project Bold—a health and human services program facility and wet labs for the science building. However, the Commonwealth will only provide $30 million for this $80 million project. Salem State must foot the remainder, which will come from the sale of campus land, campus reserves, fundraising, borrowing, and student fees. Such "gifts" from the state always include a presumption of debt and push campuses into deeper trouble.

The historical analysis outlined here helped the Massachusetts debt reveal project craft a backstory and plan for our political education campaign. Dependency on debt financing is clearly baked into Massachusetts state law. Therefore, one step towards free public higher education is to pass new state laws that allow public colleges and universities to break free from their capital debt.

THE MASSACHUSETTS DEBT REVEAL PROJECT

Joanna and Rich secured an MTA Public Relations and Organizing Grant to fund a multicampus debt

---

backlog of deferred maintenance or stop the auxiliary capital debt schemes that campuses were enmeshed in.

[11] Mass.gov/news, "Baker-Polito Administration Announces $120 Million Investment in Public Colleges and Universities," *Western Mass Economic Development Council*, April 15, 2022, https://www.westernmassedc.com.

reveal in line with MTA's Fair Share ballot initiative campaign. This campaign was a multi-union/community effort to achieve a millionaires surtax (4 percent on income and capital gains over one million dollars) earmarked for public education and transportation.

Under these auspices, the Massachusetts debt reveal project aimed to: 1) build consciousness about the amount of public campus debt across the Commonwealth and the overt and covert costs to students, faculty, staff, librarians, and community members; 2) build union power to push for increases in public spending for public higher education; and 3) to educate the voters of Massachusetts about the importance of protecting and expanding public higher education as a public good. These were interim, reformist goals to mitigate the harm of the capitalist system; they were also necessary to bring workers, students, and community members into the debt fight. We organized debt reveal activity on the thirteen Massachusetts public universities (four UMass campuses and nine state universities). Massachusetts community colleges have little capital debt and were not part of the reveal project. However, we have since been organizing with our community college colleagues to expose privatization schemes and billions of dollars of deferred maintenance.

The modest MTA grant (just $12,000) funded two statewide student coordinators ($2,000 each, 3–4 hrs/wk for one semester), nine team leaders ($500/each, 1–2 hrs/wk for one semester), and a publicity budget. By January, we had completed online interviews, met with student organizers for a biweekly orientation, supported campus team building, and offered training on the debt reveal worksheet. We engaged teams of faculty, librarians, union leaders, and students on different campuses. Each of these teams completed campus debt audits using financial statements, audits, and budget reports. The students then helped standardize the statewide information and engaged in outreach to promote the online Massachusetts campus debt reveal event.[12] This outreach took many forms, including tabling, posters, social media, campus listserv announcements, and class presentations. We also encouraged each campus team to personally invite their state legislators to attend the reveal.

Over 120 faculty, staff, students, and state legislators turned out for the online Zoom event! The student coordinators and team leaders confidently spoke about campus debt and its substantial and pervasive impacts. We revealed $3.7 billion in outstanding capital debt for the UMass System and $1.2 billion for the Mass State colleges. The average student in these two systems paid more than $2,500 each year just for their university's building debt (increasing student debt totals by about 25 percent).[13]

---

[12] Massachusetts Campus Debt Reveal Project, Spring 2022.

[13] Joanna Gonsalves, Rich Levy, Gayathri Raja, Tyler Risteen, "Campus Debt Reveal, Massachusetts Public Colleges and Universities," Massachusetts Teachers Association, September 2022.

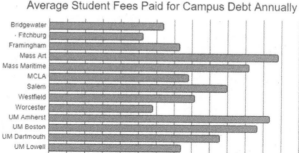

Average student fees paid toward campus debt annually ranges from approximately $1,850 to over $4,000 across the nine state colleges and four UMass campuses.

Other consequences of campus debt were also revealed:

The high cost of enrollment fees and campus housing exacerbates inequities in college access for many, particularly students of color and first-generation students.[14]

The financial burden of campus debt forced students to work more and stole time from studying and campus engagement.

It also contributed to food and housing insecurity, even after graduation. As one recent graduate testified, "Student loan debt is super

---

[14] Michael Mitchell, Michael Leachman, and Matt Saenz, "State Higher Education Funding Cuts Have Pushed Costs to Students, Worsened Inequality," Center on Budget and Policy Priorities, October 24, 2019, https://www.cbpp.org/.

stressful. Now I have a salaried job, but my loan payments are $500/month which takes a lot out of my paycheck and really decreases options for an apartment, for a car which I need to get to work and for feeding yourself every week. It really just limits your capacities in deciding things about your life every day—it determines where you live, what you do and even what you eat."

The debt reveal campus teams illustrated how debt cancellation savings could be used to lower the student debt burden and/or improve instruction. We communicated these options as quantified hypothetical scenarios. For instance, we multiplied the average annual student fee related to debt service by four (for four years of full-time enrollment) to determine possible student debt reduction. We found that average student loan indebtedness could be slashed by $7,000 to $17,000. This would be a massive improvement for Massachusetts public college student borrowers, who average $31,821 in federal loans—the tenth-highest amount in the nation.[15]

---

[15] US Department of Education, IPEDS 2023; Jeremy Thompson, "Educated and Encumbered: Student Debt Rising with Higher Education Funding Falling in Massachusetts," Massachusetts Budget and Policy Center, 2018, https://massbudget.org.

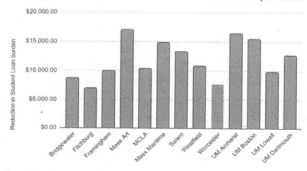

Average reduction in student loans burdens without campus debt ranges from approximately $7,000 to $17,000 across the state colleges and UMass campuses.

We then considered how many more faculty could be hired to support instructional needs without campus debt. The teams divided each campus' debt service payment by the average full-time faculty salary on their campus and the national public employee fringe rate.

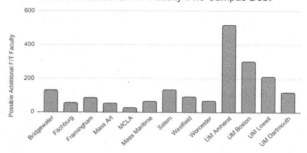

Potential increases in faculty positions ranges approximately between 12 and 120 for the state colleges and between 100 and 500 for the UMass campuses if there were no campus debt.

Theoretically, UMass Amherst could hire up to 516 more full-time faculty members if the burden of campus debt obligations were removed. This would lead to more course offerings, accommodate student schedules and interests, improve mentoring relationships and student-faculty ratios, and increase diverse voices and opinions. In debt reveal conversations, our students, alumni, and faculty were quick to share horror stories of overfilled classrooms and diminishing course offerings. One student shared that they had a strong interest in "a plethora of art, history, and science classes [that they] would have loved to take," but every semester, these classes were either not offered or filled on the first day of registration. With more money to hire faculty to cover classes, students would have more choices and a better chance at timely degree completion. More full-time positions would help reverse the trend towards low-paid, contingent faculty labor. Certainly, the freed-up monies could also go to many other scenarios. Campuses could hire more support staff, lower student fees, improve worker benefits, and provide more resources for students. Asking students and workers how to use freed-up funds is a powerful way to imagine a brighter future for public education and build collective power.

The elected officials in attendance were known advocates of public education. They had filed or supported various higher education bills but did not know the scope of public universities' debt or its direct relation to student debt. They were also unaware of the public building authorities and bondholders' grip over campus functions. A new imperative became clear: the Commonwealth needs to pay for campus capital costs and provide relief for existing campus debt. The Fair Share Amendment (i.e., the millionaires tax), if passed, could provide dedicated funding to do just that.

IMPACTS OF THE MASSACHUSETTS DEBT REVEAL PROJECT

The MTA leadership provided us with venues to educate hundreds of union members about the debt reveal and bring more colleagues into the arena. We also worked with MTA staff and Sarah Holtz, a labor reporter, to reach a more general audience in Massachusetts during the Fair Share campaign. Our debt reveal findings were widely reported in local news outlets, radio appearances, and an article in *The Nation*.[16] This publicity campaign helped connect the problem of campus debt with the push for more public higher education funding via the proposed Fair Share Amendment.

While the project may not have significantly changed rhetoric on the Fair Share campaign trail, it certainly shaped thinking within the union. For instance, MTA president Max Page helped educators connect the dots in *MTA Today:*

---

[16] Sarah Holtz, "Colleges Are in Debt, but Students Pay for It," *The Nation*, September 7, 2022, https://www.thenation.com.

The Fair Share Amendment—a fight for
racial, economic and education justice—will
guarantee that. . . we can provide even more
of what our students and our members need
to help our public schools thrive. . . . So now
it is Higher Education's time to see a renewed
investment in order to reverse the 30 percent
cut we have faced in per-student spending
in recent years. This state-imposed austerity
has led to massive student debt, the exploitation of adjunct faculty and staff, and decrepit
buildings that are slowly being repaired with
campus capital debt—which, in turn, has led
to more student debt, more exploitation of
adjuncts, and insufficient pay for higher education workers in general.[17]

You get the picture of this unvirtuous
cycle. But I want to end by lifting up what
might be the most profound and long-term
impact of winning passage of the Fair Share
Amendment. Decades of neoliberal economics have helped create a mindset that narrows
our common imagination. The ingrained
belief—hammered away at by business leaders and policymakers and the press—runs
along these lines: "There just isn't enough
money." "Belt-tightening is necessary." "I
wish we could, but. . . ." And this failure

---

[17] Max Page, "A Chance to Recapture our Political Imagination,"
MTA Today 53, no. 2 (2022): 4.

of vision eats away at what we think is possible. Fair Share can help us widen our view of the horizon, allowing us to move beyond the question: "What can we do with limited money?" Instead, we can ask: "What do students and educators need?" And: "What else, beyond our schools and colleges, do families need to lead a good life—a life filled with dignity and justice?

To our collective delight, the voters of Massachusetts approved the Fair Share ballot question! Now that public education and transportation had gained a new source of public funding, there was important policy work to do. A new multisector "Higher Ed for All"[18] campaign aimed to secure a fair share of the Fair Share to address the most pressing needs within public higher education—not campus leadership's pet projects. We set out to ensure that these new funds would (among other things) significantly reduce campus debt. We got involved with MTA working groups to draft legislation to operationalize how the Fair Share funds would be spent. The final legislative bill established a dedicated fund for campus debt relief and required a corresponding reduction in capital debt-related student fees. It also mandated that the Commonwealth must (once again) take respon-

---

[18] Massachusetts Teachers Association, "Higher Ed for All Coalition Calls for a Major Investment in Public Universities, Colleges and Students," Massachusetts Teachers Association, January 4, 2023, https://massteacher.org.

sibility for funding campus infrastructure—both academic and auxiliary.

The Massachusetts Campus Debt Report and features in Radio Boston, the *Nation*, and Public News Service meant campus presidents and chancellors could no longer pretend that campus borrowing was benign.[19] At first, campus presidents and CFOs were skeptical, defensive, and adversarial when we protested campus debt ("these were smart investments," they would quip). However, the tide turned after our Debt Reveal Report was released, and campus leadership mostly came on board. The President of the UMass system called on the Commonwealth to step up with campus capital project funding and debt relief.[20] The Council of Presidents of the State Colleges read our report and started doing their own compilation of campus debt and deferred maintenance for political advocacy.

Lastly, this pilot forced us to take a more holistic approach to debt organizing. Debt affects all campuses differently, so it is important to attend to the unequal power relations between public higher education sectors (community colleges, regional state colleges, and research universities). During an MTA debt organizing workshop, a few

---

[19] John Keenan, "Council of Presidents Remarks on Behalf of the State University System to the Board of Higher Education," Massachusetts Board of Higher Education, October 18, 2022, https://www.mass.edu.

[20] Marty Meehan, "What Does Biden's Student Debt Relief Mean for UMass Students?," *The Bill Newman Show – WHMP Radio*, August 26, 2022, https://whmp.com.

community college colleagues asked pointed questions about why they were not included in the debt reveal project. They acknowledged that community colleges in Massachusetts had very little debt; however, their campuses also struggled in the neoliberal debt system, perhaps even more than the larger institutions.

After hearing this critique, we made a pivot and started meeting with our community college peers. We learned that decades of neglect from the state, combined with community colleges' inability to borrow, had resulted in serious physical plant issues on their campuses. It often takes years for the state to approve capital projects, and these are usually piecemeal repairs, not comprehensive redesigns. Patricia Gentile, President of the Massachusetts Association of Community Colleges, succinctly described the problem in testimony to the state legislature: "Massachusetts Community Colleges have a need of more than $1.3 billion in deferred maintenance for the existing facilities among the 15 community colleges. These community colleges serve the largest portion of people of color and lower income individuals than any other higher ed sector, public or private in Massachusetts. They are the engines of opportunity for underserved students and must remain so. However, without significant capital investment, teaching spaces will continue to be outdated and of poor quality."[21] It

---

[21] Massachusetts House Committee on Bonding, State Assets, and Capital Expenditures Hearing, 191st General Session, on July 25, 2020.

is hard for community college workers not to be cynical when they hear flagship university chancellors complain about underfunding, given that the most basic infrastructure needs of the community colleges are routinely unmet.

We also learned that community college capital loans (measured in millions, not hundreds of millions or billions) have increased per-credit enrollment fees for students. At Holyoke Community College, students are paying 37 percent of a $10 million capital project through an additional per-credit fee.[22] This extra charge is roughly equivalent to each full-time HCC student buying one more expensive textbook every semester and likely gets tacked onto their student loan balance. According to a report by the Hildreth Institute, "All of these burdens are leading to negative enrollment trends that further disenfranchise communities most in need of support and investment. Community colleges saw the sharpest rates of declining enrollment—particularly among first-year Black and Latino students."[23]

Cash-strapped community colleges in need of serious campus overhauls or auxiliary services are targets for public-private partnerships (P3s) that promise new facilities (very quickly) with no

---

[22] Holyoke Community College, "Capital Improvement Plan FY 2020 – FY 2024," Holyoke Community College, October 2019, https://www.hcc.edu.

[23] Bahar Akman Imboden, "Executive Summary, Massachusetts Higher Ed: Underfunded Unaffordable and Unfair," Hildreth Institute, April 2022, https://www.hildrethinstitute.org.

impact on the campus budget. Unlike the public building authorities, P3s are for-profit entities and are allowed to generate profit with few restrictions (e.g., union wage requirements) and little state oversight (e.g., public auditing and public records access). Thus, community colleges may host expensive private student housing, fitness facilities, dining options, and conference centers on supposedly public campuses.

LESSONS LEARNED

Several points can help us scale up debt reveal organizing beyond a single campus.

SET ACHIEVABLE GOALS

Like in any organizing project, you will be more successful if you set some short-term goals to rack up early wins. It is also easier to ask people to commit to a project if there are shared interests and a common goal from the start. The specifics will develop later through ongoing dialogue. Some early demands for a campus debt project might include:

- Demanding that your state government cover the costs of capital construction and repairs;
- Demanding that your state government take over payments of existing campus capital debt;
- Pushing for federal student loan forgiveness;

- Demanding free public higher education for all residents, regardless of immigration status;
- Pushing the federal or state government to provide student grants for the full cost of attendance so students can afford the commute or to live on (or near) campus;
- Resisting the privatization of public education through P3 contracts, outsourced online education (e.g., Academic Partnerships[24]), and privately managed auxiliary campus services;
- Demanding community participation in campus or system leadership decision-making;
- Pushing for university board reform to ensure appointed or elected boards prioritize students and educational quality.

We should be wary of structures that must later be undone in the push for free higher education for all. For example, we will continue to lobby hard for statutes that ensure that the new funding stream from the millionaires tax *actually helps* our students and campuses. A campus debt relief fund must be conditioned upon lowering student fees, not freeing up budgets for the trustees' pet projects. Progress will require sustained attention, collaboration, and action among the members of the growing collective.

It took months of conversations across different campuses to gain consensus about what we

---

[24] Academic Partnerships, "Home," Academic Partnerships, n.d., https://www.academicpartnerships.com.

were fighting for (and we are still discussing the demands). Organizing around Fair Share was a great opportunity to build cross-campus and cross-labor solidarity for public higher education funding reform. We agreed that this pilot was not about skirmishes with the boss (i.e., one-off battles with a university board) or elected officials; rather, it was an entry point into organizing against existing debt structures, sparking worker and student interest, and building power to resist. Ultimately, we understood the pilot within a longer struggle—incremental progress that keeps us on course together.

WORK WITH AND FOR STUDENTS

Partnering with students on the debt reveal was transformational—their contributions and insights shaped the project and provided sharp generational contrasts. Their voices helped us understand the true meaning of "revenue bonds" in the university context (i.e., student fees secure the bonds) and that student enrollment and retention concerns are primarily about the need for student revenue to pay campus debt. In the lead-up to the debt reveal event, students translated our debt research into powerful messages, both on campus and through social media. They also generally made the project more interesting and fun. Students were also better received by legislators and campus leaders (the faculty were easily and often disregarded as merely acting in their self-interest).

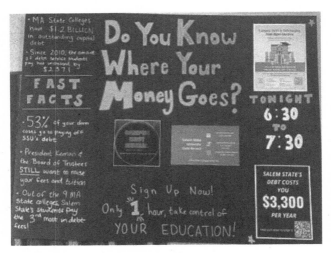

Student-made messages about campus debt.

The students explicitly linked our campus debt project to ongoing campaigns to cancel student debt. The student coordinators created and distributed an online petition for the Biden Administration to cancel debt, hosted a student debt visibility event at Framingham State, and prompted the faculty coordinators to pass student debt cancellation resolutions at the MSCA and MTA assemblies.

There were also some challenges in working with students. It always takes effort to convince anyone to care about campus debt, and it was hard to recruit students with already limited bandwidth. Students who did sign up sometimes struggled to juggle the project demands with their coursework and work schedules. A few practical steps to improve student involvement include:

- Reaching out to colleagues who are active in the union, labor studies programs, or are advisors of student clubs to help recruit students for the project;
- Designing the project with the students' academic schedule in mind—this was a semester-long project with remote meetings late in the day, and a small weekly commitment;
- Providing stipends for the students' work (another approach is to create college internships to support students engaged in debt audits);
- Stressing opportunities for resume building in recruitment materials and interviews. Our recruitment email included, "You could be a speaker at one of the workshops or even coauthor a report, publication or conference presentation on the project."

We also learned (from previous collaborations) that it is important to ask student partners what they care about and the issues they want to tackle and to make a sincere effort to support their activism. For instance, we made sure to show up for student protests of a hate speaker on Salem State's campus.[25] We provided counsel when the campus police and campus leadership enabled the speaker and gaslit the students instead of protecting the

---

[25] Joey Wolongevicz, "Column, I Am Told I Am Going to Burn in Hell on Salem State's Campus Every Week," *The Salem News*, November 2, 2021, https://www.salemnews.com.

community. We also continued to support the students' debt cancellation activism during and after the project. A few students had never been involved in a protest or campaign before, so they found this project empowering and began to see themselves as activists. We encouraged students to join us in project authorship—those who did co-led workshops, co-presented at the reveal event, gave class presentations, and made statements to the press. The two student coordinators were coauthors of the final *Debt Reveal Report*.

Student feedback suggested that it was a good experience. One student learned "so much about organizing projects and spreading information, as well as the information revealed about institutional debt." Another student was amazed to find out "how debt functions within the college system and why it is a huge issue. Also, the way in which campus leaders keep this information deeply suppressed as to continue, instead of having to dig their way out of debt and change the way they operate." As a result of these students' efforts, many other campus community members learned these things too.

UNDERSTAND YOUR STATE'S POLITICAL ECOSYSTEM

It is valuable for public university workers across a state to do an analysis and organize together. The general laws governing capital borrowing—including fundamentals like who does the borrowing, the terms of borrowing, and the vehicles (i.e., public building authorities and private corporations)—vary from state to state. In Massachusetts, elected officials have (out of apathy or disdain for public higher education) passed dozens of state laws, acts, and policies that force campuses to borrow for capital projects and relentlessly gouge their students.

In New York, the situation is different, though the problems of debt remain. The State of New York seems more progressive: dedicated income tax, part of the sales tax, and a centralized fund all pay for educational facilities (independent of the state universities' operational budgets). In FY2021, the state paid $619 million in debt service for its campus educational buildings. The catch is that politicians decide which campuses are given capital improvements and which are left to crumble. In the fall of 2022, Governor Hochul announced that four campuses would receive billions to build exceptional learning and research facilities.[26] Meanwhile, rural, regional campuses like SUNY Potsdam have structural deficits and have been put on notice for (euphemistically labeled) "realignment."[27] Therefore, New York's highly centralized and polit-

---

[26] Kathy Hochul, "Governor Hochul Announces Plan to Revitalize SUNY and Secure its Place as a Global Leader in Higher Education," New York Governor's Office, January 5, 2023, https://www.governor.ny.gov.

[27] Celia Clarke, "Facing $3 Million Deficit, SUNY Potsdam Weighs Cuts to Majors Amidst Leadership Transitions," North Country Public Radio, August 10, 2022, https://www.northcountrypublicradio.org

icized capital financing means that local campuses lose their autonomy to decide their futures.

Like Massachusetts, New York does not support campus auxiliary facilities.[28] This has given rise to the powerful Dormitory Authority State of New York (DASNY), the largest public borrowing authority in the country.[29] Working with our colleagues in the SUNY system, we found DASNY's reporting to be particularly untransparent, making it difficult for campus communities to see debt's impacts. However, with some patience, DASNY's financial statements revealed that students are charged very high fees for the residence halls and other services because of debt. For instance, SUNY dormitory revenue in FY 2019 was $593 million, of which $159 million went to pay debt service (27 percent of students' dorm fees).[30]

Working across campuses allows us to compare better and worse practices to understand what can and must change. For example, the Commonwealth of Maryland judiciously places state revenue surpluses in a rainy day fund and uses those funds for

[28] New York State, "Executive Budget, Capital Program and Financing Plan FY 2023," New York State, n.d., https://www.budget.ny.gov.

[29] DANSY, "2022 Annual Report," Dormitory Authority State of New York, n.d., https://www.dasny.org.

[30] State University of New York, "SUNY Bond Official Statement, Series 2021A, 2021B, and 2021C," Electronic Municipal Market Access, n.d., https://emma.msrb.org.

public education capital projects.[31] Meanwhile, the Commonwealth of Massachusetts unwisely returns such surpluses to the taxpayers.[32] Working across campuses helps to contextualize our demands and targets.

You do not need a statewide union campaign to start cross-campus organizing. It can be as simple as colleagues from different campuses deciding to do this work together. Even where public higher education is decentralized (every campus has separate finances and lenders, and each campus union is a separate bargaining entity), organizing does not have to be decentralized. For instance, a group of Oregon educators, motivated by other campus debt reveals, banded together to start organizing against debt in 2022.

KEEP AN EYE ON THE HORIZON

Nearly all public higher education systems in the United States are encumbered with capital debt. Students and campus workers across the nation are paying the price—in different ways—for campus debt traps. Debt financing turns our campuses into businesses that generate enough revenue for operations *and* significant (current and future) capital

---

[31] Brianna January, "State Closes with $2B Surplus, School Construction to Get Boost," *Conduit Street*, September 15, 2022, https://conduitstreet.mdcounties.org.

[32] Jason Wright, "A Blast from the Past: Reagan-Era Tax Law Hits Hard," Massachusetts Budget and Policy Center, August 5, 2022, https://massbudget.org.

debt obligations. This financialization pushes campuses to profit from student enrollment, leading university trustees and regents to value profitable professional degree programs over liberal arts programs. Students also worry about their loan debt and gravitate toward degrees they think will give them a greater return on investment as they start their careers. This is a significant threat to liberal education (whether it is true or not).

More broadly, debt financing undermines our universities' missions and hurts the communities we serve. Resistance starts by investigating and questioning university debt, and then by organizing against the structures that perpetuate it. Scaling up the work across campuses can only build strength for the long fight to achieve free public higher education.

CHAPTER SIX
FIGHTING THE DEBT ECONOMY
FROM THE PEOPLE'S UNIVERSITY:
THE CASE OF THE UNIVERSITY OF
PUERTO RICO

This chapter positions universities as ideal sites of resistance against the debt economy. Its case study illustrates the extreme effects of capitalism and the disciplinary measures of debt repayment at the University of Puerto Rico (UPR). The university itself does not have significant institutional debt and its students do not suffer from massive student loan debt (as described in previous chapters). However, the austerity measures imposed on UPR mirror the situation at US public higher education institutions, as Puerto Rico's debt repayment has halved the state's contribution to UPR.

We consider why the "people's university" is the main target of the Financial Oversight and Management Board (FOMB) imposed by the US Congress to restructure Puerto Rico's debt. It explains how to organize against the debt economy from within the university and build up resistance beyond the university. The debt economy is sustained by a hegemonic assertion that all debts must be paid. "Debt moralists" argue that paying debt is a moral responsibility, the only acceptable outcome. When you owe something, you need to pay it! We offer something different, something that rejects the uncritical acceptance of debt repayment and argues for debt cancellation.

Plato's *Republic*, considered by many as the beginning of political philosophy, discusses the question of what justice is. When Cephalus explains that "justice is telling the truth and paying your debts," Socrates argues against debt repayment and gives him specific examples of when debt repayment is not the right thing to do.[1] George Caffentzis' reading of *The Republic* argues that debt repayment does not equal justice, especially when the repayment of a debt will lead to death and unjust consequences.[2] Here, Caffentzis is referring to student loan debt, but Puerto Rico's unaudited and illegitimate debt also leads to death and unjust consequences. Socrates also refused to pay debts to a mad credi-

---

[1] "Suppose, for example, a friend who had lent us a weapon were to go mad and then ask for it back, surely anyone would say we ought not to return it. It would not be 'right' to do so; nor yet to tell the truth without reserve to a madman. No, it would not. Right conduct, then, cannot be defined as telling the truth and restoring anything we have been trusted with." Plato, *The Republic*, 331c, translated by Paul Shorey (1857–1934), *Plato in Twelve Volumes*. Cambridge, Massachusetts: Harvard University Press, 1929.

[2] George Caffentzis, "Platos Republic and Student Loan Debt Refusal," in *UniConflicts in Spaces of Crisis* (Thessaloniki: Encounters and Conflicts in the City Group, 2016), 44–9.

tor who could harm themselves and others. What is capitalism, if not madness? Capitalism's contradictions are beyond belief—it seeks ecological destruction for growth, it sees austerity as progress, it uses disasters as opportunities, and it denies basic human rights to make the rich richer and the poor poorer.[3] In such a context, can debt repayment ever be moral, especially in the colony of Puerto Rico? For Zambrana, "debt functions as a form of coloniality. . . debt actualizes, updates, reinstalls the colonial condition."[4] We must ask: 1) who owes whom in a colonial relationship, 2) is debt legitimate when it originated from a denial of human rights, 3) is it ethical to pay an unaudited debt, and 4) what happens when debt repayment has a human cost.

In Puerto Rico, the fight for public education goes hand-in-hand with decolonization. The country has recently been struck with the governance of unelected Wall Street bankers, the aftermath of two hurricanes in 2017, a string of earthquakes in early 2020, two years of shutdowns due to the pandemic, and another hurricane in 2022. Draconian budget cuts have slashed and privatized health, education, social services, agriculture, energy, land, and infrastructure. Yet, Puerto Rico must still pay an unaudited debt to Wall Street vulture funds.

---

[3] David Harvey, *Marx, Capital and the Madness of Economic Reason* (Oxford: Oxford University Press, 2017).

[4] Rocío Zambrana, *Colonial Debts: The Case of Puerto Rico* (Durham: Duke University Press, 2021), 10.

This is disaster capitalism in its prime and colonialism at its worst—it is not ethical nor fair and has an enormous human cost. The struggle to survive the debt economy defines the lives of Puerto Ricans. It is a question of "to survive or to live?" To be resilient or to be resistant?

Governments that impose austerity and insurmountable debt are aiding the creditors and bankers, not the people they represent. When governments fail their main responsibility of service to the people, the people respond to that betrayal in different acts of subversion and resistance. As Zambrana explains, "These protests employ tactics of subversion, inversion, refusal, and rescue/occupation aimed at interrupting the operation of debt."[5] Such acts of subversion have taken place within the University of Puerto Rico, where students and university workers defend the university and advance Puerto Ricans' larger fight against the debt economy.

THE MADNESS OF DEBT IN PUERTO RICO

Puerto Rico's debt is part of the neoliberal agenda that has pushed public universities to take on additional loans in response to plummeting funding. Puerto Rico has a public debt of $74 billion in outstanding bonds and $49 billion owed in pensions. It defaulted on its debt payments in January 2016. In a shocking moment, the then-governor of Puerto

---

[5] Zambrana, *Colonial Debts*, 12.

Rico, Alejandro García Padilla, told cameras, "It's very simple. We don't have money to pay."[6] While Padilla spent the following months trying to roll back this stance (bravery may not have been a factor at play), his public words made it real—not paying was a possibility. Those words were enough to rattle the crate. Who was this governor of a forsaken colony in the Caribbean to question the idea of paying a debt to Wall Street?

The possibility of not paying the debt stirred the US Congress into political action. They introduced PROMESA—the Puerto Rico Oversight, Management, and Economic Stability Act,[7] a slow death sentence for Puerto Ricans. In June 2016, the Financial Oversight Management Board (FOMB) was established to manage the country's economy and restructure the debt. The FOMB—colloquially, "*la Junta*"—is a group of unelected Wall Street bankers who now have control over every financial decision in the country.

The FOMB, the US Congress, and Puerto Rico's government have no interest in auditing the country's debt, as this would reveal its culprits and illegalities. While it would seem reasonable to investigate and trace every cent of the alleged $74 billion bill, capitalism is madness, and no one (in power) has seriously questioned how it came to

---

[6] Mary Williams Walsh, "Puerto Rico Defaults on Debt Payments," New York Times, January 4, 2016, https://www.nytimes.com.

[7] US Congress, Senate, *Puerto Rico Oversight, Management, and Economic Stability Act*, S 2328, 114th Congress, 1st session, introduced in Senate, November 19, 2015.

be or who was involved. Where did this money come from? Where did it go? The people of Puerto Rico surely cannot point to any investments in public goods. The Puerto Rico Commission for the Comprehensive Audit of the Public Debt's[8] Pre-Audit Survey Report explains many aspects of its illegality. For example, the Constitution of the Commonwealth of Puerto Rico prohibits the government from borrowing to cover budget deficits, but this was done several times. It also states that Puerto Rico cannot take out any debt that would make it spend more than 15 percent of internal Treasury revenues on General Obligation Debt— yet it has. It also prohibits issuing notes lasting more than thirty years and the "scoop and toss" practice of refinancing debt when it comes due instead of paying it.[9] In many ways, the debt is illegal, making debt repayment little more than money laundering authorized within the colonial condition.

This is not the US Congress' first experience in forcing austerity for debt repayment. There is a playbook that gets applied repeatedly across time and place, but that primarily affects Black and Brown communities like Detroit, Puerto Rico, and the Global South. In the early 2010s, the City of Detroit had $18 billion of debt, including outstanding bonds and unfunded liabilities to its worker

---

[8] In Spanish, it is *Frente Ciudadano por la Auditoría de la Deuda*.

[9] These are just a few examples of the illegality of Puerto Rico's $74 billion debt. Puerto Rico Commission for the Comprehensive Audit of the Public Debt, "Pre-audit Survey Report," *Centro de Periodismo Investigativo*, n.d., https://periodismoinvestigativo.com.

pensions and retiree healthcare. The municipality filed for Chapter 9 bankruptcy and was stripped of control over its finances. Instead, emergency financial manager Kevin Orr was placed in charge. There are parallels in Puerto Rico (though Chapter 9 is reserved for state and local governments, not island colonies). Title III of PROMESA Law offers bankruptcy-like proceedings to restructure the debt, but the bankruptcy proceedings and debt repayment are not negotiated by the people (via their elected officials). Rather, the FOMB "represents" Puerto Rico in negotiations with the bondholders and vulture funds. Unelected bankers on both sides of the table get to divvy up an unaudited and illegitimate $74 billion tab. The fact that the FOMB decides Puerto Ricans' futures reveals a clear lack of democracy and colonial abuse that normalizes the debt economy. Over five years, the FOMB has imposed severe austerity measures affecting essential services, with one of their main targets being defunding the University of Puerto Rico.[10]

Debt crises are the result of undemocratic political decisions as much as economic ones. Puerto Rico's situation perfectly illustrates how the creditor-debtor relationship is undemocratic and colonial. Puerto Ricans are forced to pay a debt that we did not take on. Political decisions (some illegal) were made without the consent of the people,

---

[10] "PROMESA Has Failed: How a Colonial Board Is Enriching Wall Street and Hurting Puerto Ricans," The Center for Popular Democracy, September 24, 2021, https://www.populardemocracy.org.

who must now cough up $74 billion. Furthermore, those 'representing' the people's best interest in the debt restructuring are US Congress-installed Wall Street bankers who do not care about the human costs of repayment. Call Socrates, the situation is mad!

THE SIGNIFICANCE OF THE UNIVERSITY OF PUERTO RICO

The University of Puerto Rico was founded in 1903, only a few years after the US invasion of the island in 1898. It is now the primary public university serving the people of Puerto Rico, pursuing knowledge, and contributing to the development of culture by making knowledge accessible to society. Initially, only the privileged few could study at UPR; however, it became a university of the masses in the second half of the twentieth century. UPR's eleven campuses on the main island make education accessible in all geographical areas. It is the country's most prestigious university and requires the highest scores for entry. It also boasts the lowest cost to students and the highest retention and graduation rates. UPR is a research hub, with 75 percent of research in PR coming from the university system. It is also the main healthcare provider in the country since the best hospitals are part of UPR's medical school. Other important services include the Puerto Rico Seismic Network (PRSN), the Agriculture Network, and the Legal Assistance Clinic. Some of the most talented individuals from various fields of expertise, such as art, writing, economics, painting, law, music, science, philosophy, engineering, and medicine teach at UPR.

The university is also an economic multiplier: $1.56 is produced for every $1 invested in UPR.[11] Here, we should be skeptical of neoliberal discourses that see universities as economic multipliers and education as a mere return on investment. Clearly, universities are essential spaces of society regardless of their 'return on investment.' However, the dismantling of UPR seems to even contradict neoliberalism's own logic. If Puerto Rico is experiencing such an economic crisis, why defund an institution that can help the country overcome its financial crisis? Why insist on this particular course of madness? The answer is simple: the FOMB and the US Congress do not want Puerto Rico to overcome its financial crisis. They want to keep us in debt. Debt keeps us in check, controls us, maintains the colonial power relation, and legitimizes a board of unelected officials deciding how to (not) allocate funding.

The University of Puerto Rico has been a stronghold of anticolonial resistance for a long time. In fact, many political struggles during the second half of the twentieth century took place at UPR. During this time, students were persecuted, illegally profiled, and even killed by the police. To secure UPR's

[11] José I. Alameda-Lozada and Alfredo González-Martínez, "El Impacto Socioeconómico del Sistema de la Universidad de Puerto Rico," *Estudios Técnicos*, April 2017, https://www.estudiostecnicos.com.

autonomy, a no-confrontation policy was enacted, prohibiting the Puerto Rican police from entering UPR's campuses. Instead, UPR has its own security guards, and conflicts must be resolved through the *Junta Coordinadora de Seguridad.*

UPR has hosted many national protests, including protests against the Vietnam and Iraq wars, a movement to get the US Navy out of Vieques and Culebra (1979–2001), antiprivatization struggles, rallies for Puerto Rico's independence, anticorruption protests, Ricky Renuncia protests (2019), and strikes against the FOMB in 2017 and 2021. UPR students and the university community have always been part of Puerto Rico's different resistance fronts. As a result, the university has become a site of social justice and resistance. It is a place of refuge in a country that is in debt and crisis. Despite the history of police brutality and murder dating back to the 1950s, the students continue to fight for a better future for their country.

Unfortunately, UPR has become one of the FOMB's main targets. From 2005 to 2016, UPR enrolled approximately 62–66,000 students. However, after the FOMB was established in 2016, student enrollment decreased significantly. By 2022, only 41,783 students remained enrolled. The government uses the "debt" as an excuse to impose austerity measures on everything that does not align with the neoliberal agenda, which primarily favors the rich. Programs that are not deemed "profitable"—such as humanities, gender studies, and ethnic studies—are often the first to be cut. By slashing at UPR, the FOMB diminishes the university community and reduces Puerto Rico's ability to fight capitalism and poverty. UPR is a social project that demands human rights and educates and serves the people of Puerto Rico with many public services. It allows students to climb the socioeconomic ladder and, sometimes, to escape poverty. In many ways, the University of Puerto Rico is a symbol and a scenario of social change and justice.

Debt has been the perfect excuse to impose austerity measures on everything that deviates from the neoliberal agenda. This austerity strikes stronger against Black, Brown, and non-cis male bodies; as Zambrana notes, "The operation of debt involves expulsion, dispossession, and precarization through which race/gender/class hierarchies are deepened, intensified, posited anew. Debt lands, as Verónica Gago and Luci Cavallero suggest, on bodies and populations."[12] The connection between life and debt is crucial in organizing higher education communities and finding ways to fight for public funding and debt cancellation.

PROMESA-ERA BUDGET CUTS AT UPR

When Puerto Rico defaulted on its loan, UPR's institutional debt was a manageable $450 million, and the university was not defaulting on its payments. In 2017, the FOMB lumped UPR's debt together with the country's general debt,

---

[12] Zambrana, *Colonial Debts*, 10.

enabling the FOMB to impose budget cuts and austerity measures on UPR as if it were defaulting. The budget cuts imposed by the FOMB have now far surpassed the original institutional debt. They have resulted in frozen employee salaries, increased healthcare costs, eliminated tuition waivers for children and family members, increased workload and class sizes, and the elimination of research and development funding (while keeping the normal requirements of academic work). The retirement pension plan is now also being directly threatened.[13] Finally, the FOMB-imposed budget cuts have increased the number of adjunct professors: in 2022, adjuncts constituted 44 percent of UPR's faculty, with more than 60 percent of these adjuncts on part-time contracts with salaries below the poverty line (less than $17,000 annually).[14]

---

[13] The FOMB is supposed to limit its jurisdiction to financial oversight; however, it intervenes in all government decisions. For example, a FOMB letter to Governor Pedro Pierluisi on April 22, 2022 references the University of Puerto Rico and the Defined Benefits Pension Plan for its employees. The retirement plan is completely outside of the FOMB's jurisdiction; nevertheless, the letter states: "50 percent of the increased appropriation will be conditioned on UPR closing its Defined Benefit plan to new members and successfully transferring non-vested employees to a Defined Contribution plan." The FOMB officially has oversight over every financial decision in Puerto Rico. It also has oversight over everything else by way of blackmail.

[14] Part-time faculty with PhDs at UPR earn approximately $681 per credit per year. If they teach a "full workload" of 24 credits per academic year, but on different campuses, it only counts as two part-time positions, so they earn approximately $16,344 per academic year. This is far below the poverty line and minimum wage.

Historically, Pell Grants covered the cost of tuition, books, housing, and some daily costs for undergraduate students. Student loans were not the norm. However, over the years, tuition costs have increased drastically, and it is now impossible for many students to pay for their education. Furthermore, thirteen of the sixteen tuition waiver types (e.g., for athletes and other student activities) have been eliminated. In 2018, the general credit cost was $57; in 2023, it had increased to $157. This 175 percent increase in tuition over just five years has dramatically lowered student enrollment. Students can no longer live off the Pell Grants alone, so they take on several jobs while studying. UPR's reduced student body is overworked and part of Puerto Rico's low-wage working class.

According to the law, UPR is supposed to receive 9.6 percent of Puerto Rico's revenue.[15] The government's revenue has increased over the last four years, but the FOMB has indiscriminately reduced the university's budget. With no evidence, the FOMB argues that 9.6 percent of state funding for UPR is too high.[16] However, the average contribution to higher education in all fifty states was 9.2 percent of revenue, as reported by the 2020 census;[17] in 2022, the average state contribution

[15] Law #2 of 1966, Article 3.

[16] Rima Brusi Gil, "La lógica de los recortes a la UPR," *El Nuevo Día*, December 2, 2021, https://www.elnuevodia.com.

[17] Urban Institute, "Higher Education Expenditures," *Urban Institute*, n.d., https://www.urban.org.

to higher education institutions was 11.8 percent (Figure 7).[18]

State investments in higher education as a percentage of the general fund (2022).

After the FOMB-imposed budget cuts, Puerto Rico could only invest 4.9 percent—the lowest of all the states. With only half of its legally entitled budget, decay is visible in UPR's buildings, classrooms, and campus infrastructure (especially after the hurricanes and earthquakes). The FOMB's claim that Puerto Rico spent too much is patently false since the legally required 9.6 percent is actually below the national average. The FOMB breaks the law because it can—it is above the law. Capitalism and colonialism intersect to dismantle UPR and deprive Puerto Ricans of their right to higher education.

---

[18] University of Puerto Rico, "Memorial de Presupuesto Año Fiscal 2023–2024," *Universidad de Puerto Rico ante Comisión de Hacienda y Presupuesto de la Cámara de Representantes de Puerto Rico,* April 27, 2023, https://s3.documentcloud.org.

"BACK TO THE FUTURE"

UPR's experience neither fully predicts the future nor repeats the past of public colleges and universities on the US mainland. The two contexts are not comparable in a linear manner; instead, they exist within a capitalist cycle of debt and madness akin to "back to the future."

The University of Puerto Rico has been a hub of social justice and political resistance since its inception. However, it is currently facing numerous challenges that threaten its existence. The past six years of economic turmoil, political unrest, climate disasters, and a global health crisis have taken a toll on UPR, affecting its faculty, students, and staff. Despite this, the community has not given up and continues to fight back. Though fewer in numbers and exhausted, they persistently defend UPR for future generations. UPR serves as an inspiring model to empower other colleges and universities in the US to become sites of resistance and free from debt. If higher education communities in the US keep organizing against debt and keep building a movement to break down the debt economy, colleges and universities can live up to what Assata Shakur calls their "tremendous revolutionary potential. . . to the problem, working collectively (we) can solve it. There is a great need for a student movement to be built, based not just on students' rights but on human rights." We seek a university that is a seed of change for society. This juncture in time is promising since higher education communities in the US are waking up to imagine and organize for a different university.

The future of public universities in the US will be bright if we continue to organize ourselves effectively. However, the higher education debt crisis is a cause for concern and serves as a warning for the future of the University of Puerto Rico. Currently, UPR and its students are resisting the option of taking on debt. The 9.6 percent formula provided a sufficient budget for UPR. Until recently, UPR students were able to study at a low cost, with their Pell Grants covering their tuition and living expenses. It was not common for students to take out loans. However, due to the defunding and hostile attacks by the Financial Oversight and Management Board on UPR, the institution may have to take on institutional debt and increase tuition even more. This could force students to take on debt to complete their studies, like the situation in many US colleges and universities. In this way, FOMB's actions under PROMESA are pushing UPR towards a debt crisis, similar to what US higher education is currently experiencing.

In Puerto Rico, we need to continue organizing to prevent institutional debt and student loan debt. A junior at UPR Mayagüez shares their thoughts: "This year, I decided to take up a student loan; it's only me and my mom. I could not afford it and I could not keep up with work and study. I didn't want to, but I had to." Even with all the FOMB's pressures, students still are inclined against debt. Many prefer the sacrifice of multiple jobs, like this freshman student at UPR Cayey: "My Pell Grant doesn't cover everything, and my parents cannot afford to pay for all my expenses; that's why I have two part-time jobs. I don't want to take out loans, but it's frustrating seeing some of my grades and knowing that I could have done better if I had more time and didn't have to work. I am tempted, but I don't want to get into debt." Debt is part of daily life in Puerto Rico—public debt is evident in every aspect of Puerto Ricans' lives. Thus, it is not surprising that students are hesitant to take on debt. In this sense, UPR is not yet a community of debtors, but it could become one if the FOMB stays in power.

BREAKING THE CYCLE OF DEBT

The practice of defunding higher education creates a cycle of debt and repayment that negatively affects both institutions and individuals, regardless of the human cost. It is imperative that we collectively break this cycle of debt and death. In Puerto Rico, this means getting the FOMB out of power. Breaking the capitalist cycle requires Puerto Ricans to break with colonialism because our colonial condition is what sustains the madness of a FOMB misrepresenting PR in the restructuring of its debt.

In the US colony of Puerto Rico, one subversive interruption to the colonial paradigm centers historical debts over financial debts. This "invert[s] the position of the creditor and the debtor, inverting who owes what to whom by taking back what is owed. . . posit[s] life beyond the strictures of private property, challenging private property itself. . . generate[s] infrastructures for a life yet to come from within material conditions here and now. . . affirm[s] that we, in fact, are all heirs taking back rather than paying back."[19] Interrupting the cycle demands taking a step back to look at the historical debts between the US and Puerto Rico to ask who really owes whom. This is how we might shift the paradigm to challenge capitalism and colonialism and demand debt cancellation, taking back what we are owed.

In the US, breaking the cycle means organizing campus communities to become sites of resistance. It requires us to push for the university we envision, a university that is for the people, with free tuition, academic freedom, and autonomy, a place of hope and growth. Capitalism denies this possibility by perpetuating debt. Public higher education institutions in the US do not have Puerto Rico's colonial debt, but they can still ask the question of who owes whom. For too long, higher education in the US has been structured as a privilege for those who can pay it or who are willing to take on debt. Fighting against the debt culture is taking back the fundamental right to education from those who profit from it—the same Wall Street players control the debt economy on the mainland. We must ensure that everyone has full access to higher education,

---

[19] Zambrana, *Colonial Debts*, 16.

especially those who have been denied it due to systemic inequalities perpetuated by capitalism.

THE HISTORY OF FUTURE STRUGGLES:

UPR Cayey professors interrupt graduation with a message for students—"Defend YOUR University" and "Restitute the 9.6 percent"—and receive a standing ovation.

GO BEYOND CAMPUS

Academic communities sometimes alienate themselves from wider social struggles, which ultimately benefits the neoliberal agenda. Mobilizations at UPR are not limited to university issues; they include other demonstrations against austerity measures that affect the quality of life and human rights in the country. Participating in wider struggles fosters a collective understanding of the debt economy. For example, the university community was present in the fight against LUMA's contract to privatize the public electric grid, yearly May Day demonstrations, and teachers' mobilizations to defend their pension plan. Going beyond campus helps people understand that campus debt is part of a bigger monster.

The 2017 student strike at the University of Puerto Rico was a great example of the power of student strikes and walkouts. The entire university community came together to participate in the strike in various ways. In such strikes, students halt all activities on their campus until their demands are met. UPR students voted to strike in student assemblies and then began blocking all entrances to the campuses. This occupation put pressure on university administrators to negotiate with the student demands. In 2017, UPR students went on a three-month-long strike due to the introduction of the PROMESA Law, the FOMB, and government bankruptcy. Their main demands included zero cuts to UPR's budget, no tuition increases, a university reform led by the university community, and a public debt audit. In particular, the demand for an audit went beyond the university space. The strike was officially approved by an in-person student assembly that included the entire UPR system, the School of Plastic Arts, the Conservatory of Music, and UPR High School. The historic strike saw the participation of over 10,000 students who gathered at the Roberto Clemente Coliseum in San Juan. UPR professors' general assembly also decided to support the student strike and were present at the gates, adding demands for better adjunct working conditions and a Citizen's Front for the Debt Audit. The HEEND, a union that represents nonteaching employees, also participated in the strike. Despite their differences, students, faculty, and employees have always united to defend UPR.

The students' predictions about the negative implications of the FOMB were prophetic. All the things they had warned about unfolded. Although they could not prevent the budget cuts, they were able to lessen the impact. Furthermore, the proposed tuition increase for that year was cancelled, and a multisector committee was established to work on university reform and address governance issues from the grassroots. Unfortunately, the administration failed to convene this committee, but professors, employees, and students took the initiative to convene themselves and began working towards the goals.[20]

---

[20] Comisión Multisectoral de Reforma Universitaria, "CMRU – Comisión Multisectorial de Reforma Universitaria, Facebook, n.d., https://www.facebook.com.

In November 2021, students at UPR went on strike for a month to protest against the Debt Restructuring Plan proposed by the government, the FOMB, hedge funds, and bondholders. They demanded its cancellation. This strike was organized in collaboration with the *Frente Ciudadano por la Auditoría de la Deuda* [Citizens Debt Audit Front]. These two incidents show how UPR can become a site of resistance on issues that extend beyond the boundaries of the university.

MOBILIZE STUDENTS, MOBILIZE EVERYONE

Students are the spark! However, compared to their counterparts in Puerto Rico and Latin America, students on the mainland are less likely to participate in strikes and walkouts. One possible reason is the lack of information available to them. Many students are unaware of what demands they can make. Effective political action often requires people to take these steps:

1. Know about debt and become informed;
2. Recognize how debt affects you;
3. Identify specific demands regarding debt cancelation;
4. Agitate others to go through these steps to join the fight against debt;
5. Act, join others in direct actions to get your demands met, including knowing the agents and how to pressure university administrators.

College campuses and universities are communities of debtors, and campus debt reveals can spark this process and mobilize students. Professors can also be agents of change in their classrooms and beyond.

Sometimes, student life is filled with superficial social activities that alienate students from political action. Dorm life is a very expensive bubble that separates student life from society outside of campus. We must demand a change in university culture and encourage political involvement from our communities of debtors. Organizing leisure activities that relate to the topic of debt or the effects of debt culture in academia could change the alienating culture on our campuses. Movie screenings, forums, chalk graffiti, and poster parties can help the university community discuss social issues and politicize campus life. Use five minutes of your classes to discuss important issues—students will appreciate the possibility of informed dialogue. Inspiring students beyond the content of their classes can help change campus culture and motivate political action.

SUPPORT COLLECTIVE BARGAINING FOR ALL SECTORS!

Because debt is a labor issue, collective bargaining and organized worker power are essential. Threats to working conditions have pushed many different organizations within UPR to unionize and seek contract bargaining with near-universal support from their workers (under PR Law #130). Three unions—HEEND, UBOS, and FLEURUM—all handily won union elections (HEEND with 98.94 percent, UBOS with 99 percent, and FLEURUM with 95 percent) in 2022.[21] The APPU—Association of University Professors of Puerto Rico—won union elections by 97 percent in October 2023, becoming the first university professors' union in Puerto Rico. These groups are independent unions with no connections to other international or US unions. Rank-and-file unions are essential in getting things done. All unions should be rank-and-file and, if they are not, we must change them from within since unions provide organizing structures in the fight against debt.

All workers employed at the University of Puerto Rico share the same pension and healthcare plan. They have come together to defend their pension system and health insurance benefits through protests, mobilizations, and grassroots lobbying in the legislature. Although these issues may seem minor when compared to the larger economic challenges faced by the country, they are important resistance fronts that highlight the urgency of improving working conditions for university workers.

---

[21] HEEND is the *Hermandad de Empleados Excentos No Docentes* [Union of Nonacademic Employees], UBOS is the *Union of Bona Fide Security Officers*, and FLEURUM is the *Federación Laborista de Empleados del Recinto Universitario de Mayagüez,* a union of workers from the Mayagüez campus.

Retirement and healthcare cuts are directly linked to the austerity measures imposed by the FOMB's insistence on paying an unaudited debt. Keeping a bargaining contract that ensures these benefits is essential if people are to defend their rights. Every small victory must be celebrated.

One strategy to mobilize people linked the loss of job benefits to the more general fight to restore UPR's funding and against the country's debt payment. University workers from the eleven campuses came together during informative forums on these issues. In general, tenured professors' salaries are higher than other employees and they enjoy certain privileges that make them feel above the working class. These professors only started to understand their position within a salaried working class after we organized forums on labor issues (e.g., retirement and healthcare) and how austerity threatens all of us. APPU's educational campaigns visited the eleven campuses to talk about defending our pension plan with all workers (not only professors). The discussions were diverse, but workers realized that their collective benefits were the same, regardless of their specific jobs. Such work connects people to the bigger struggle and strengthens the union's fight—the fight of an entire working class against the debt economy.

During the APPU's election campaign, professors sat down with the student unions to discuss the importance of having a union of professors. We talked about how it could benefit our common struggle against budget cuts, and the students were enthusiastic about our campaign and actively participated in it. The student unions also showed their support by sending letters to the campus community. On the day of the union elections, several professors were moved when they walked into their classrooms and found that students had written messages of support on the chalkboards. This definitely helped professors to go out and vote. Other unions recorded messages of support as part of the campaign. We were able to get the message out clearly: debt is a labor issue, and we need unionized forces to claim the university that we all deserve.

PROTEST AND PROPOSE

The university community's struggles and protests have been accompanied by proposals. The New University Reform Law was created by the university community to address governance problems after the 2017 strike. It reorganized university governance, dealt with corruption in the appointment of university administrators, and limited the state's influence in UPR's administration. The Senate of Puerto Rico failed to pass the law (by one vote) in January 2022 due to FOMB pressure. However, the mobilization and grassroots lobbying were so strong that we will get a second chance to present it before the House of Representatives in 2024. If approved, UPR's funding would be restored to 9.6 percent, and the problem of partisan political interference would be drastically reduced.[22] New democratic administrative processes would respond to bottom-up politics. Of course, no reform can solve all issues, but it is a front of resistance that could provide resources and strategies for building the university that people want and need while taking power away from capital financiers and politicians.

The APPU started a media campaign explaining why UPR is essential for Puerto Rico and should be removed from the PROMESA bankruptcy process, fiscal plans, and the FOMB's supervision. The 2019 campaign—*#uprMIuniversidad* (#UPRis*MY*university)—included radio spots with testimonials from people who had never studied or worked at UPR but had their lives changed by the university in some way. Additionally, murals were designed and painted on the campuses, merchants near UPR campuses signed onto official opposition to UPR funding cuts, and a Change.org petition to restore the 9.6 percent formula gathered more than 35,000 signatures in a few days. This campaign strengthened people's ties to UPR as a public

---

[22] A major problem at UPR is that the governor appoints the members of the board of trustees and the president of the university. The president then appoints the eleven chancellors, and the chancellors appoint the deans. Therefore, administrators respond to the political party in power, not to the university community. Under this new university law, appointments would have to come from a pool of candidates previously vetted by the university community. The community will also have the power to remove chancellors and deans to ensure more democratic governance.

university. It also connected the university sector to the general population.

Another example of protesting and proposing comes from the people's audit of Puerto Rico's debt. In response to the FOMB, government, and US Congress' refusal to audit the debt, the people organized into a citizen's audit front [*Frente Ciudadano por la Auditoría de la Deuda*].[23] The university community is heavily involved in the Frente and their incredible auditing work. With each new restructuring plan, the Frente activates to inform the public of its consequences; students and faculty help disseminate the information between campuses. The Frente has several economists and lawyers but also has nonspecialists to help communicate, mobilize, and question the debt. The student strikes of 2017 and 2021 used specific claims gathered from the Frente's work.

REFORM FOR REAL CHANGE: LESSONS FROM UPR

The movement against the debt economy implies that public universities should not only be places of education but also sites of social change. Reforms alone are not enough, but cancelling all student and campus debt puts us on the path to structural change and a debt-free society. Our demand for full state funding for public higher education and free tuition for all is rooted in the belief that educa-

---

[23] AuditoraYa.org, "Who We Are," n.d., http://www.auditoriaya.org.

tion should be a common good. However, fighting for a fully state-funded public university should not mean trading what we have for a tyranny of the state. Anticapitalist agendas should fight the hegemonic logic that those who provide capital (whether venture funds or the state) should be entitled to fully control our institutions.

A fully state-funded, tuition-free, and autonomous university is not reformist but rather revolutionary; we should take steps to ensure autonomy, even within current reforms. Many lessons learned from UPR are examples of how reform can be part of structural change. First, university governance should be restructured as bottom-up politics to ensure that administrators answer to the university community, not financiers and politicians. Secondly, we should stabilize public colleges and universities' budgets by guaranteeing a fixed percentage of state appropriations, regardless of political variations. Thirdly, nonconfrontational policies should be implemented to avoid state intervention in university conflicts and protect the university community and its sites of resistance. For example, UPR's nonconfrontation policy prohibits police and special forces from entering university grounds when there are strikes and protests unless the *Junta Coordinadora de Seguridad* (composed of representatives from all university sectors) invites the police in.

CREATIVE RESISTANCE AND MAKING SPACE FOR JOY

Creativity is essential to motivate people to join the fight. In the summer of 2019, Puerto Ricans took over the streets in (an ultimately successful) protest to demand the resignation of the governor of Puerto Rico, Ricardo Roselló. These protests included many art forms and turned hobbies into acts of protest alongside the usual manifestations of political opposition. There was *"perreo combativo,"* a sexually explicit way of dancing to reggaeton music, in front of the Cathedral and next to the governor's house. The massive demonstrations also included kayaking protests, cycling protests, horse-riding protests, and aerial yoga on the highways. This explosion of creativity opened ludic experiences within the resistance and brought the masses out. Debt can be an arid topic, thus, fighting campus debt requires creativity to move people into action.

There is much to learn from UPR students. They have learned to enjoy the struggle and have a good time, even when on strike. They befriend the people they fight alongside—comrades become your community. The camaraderie alleviates fatigue and helps people fight another day. Joy does not disrespect the cause; on the contrary, it helps us carry on amidst apathy and burnout. As organizers, we must plan activities that simply get people together and serve as spaces to vent and maintain a routine (e.g., Coffee Tuesdays and Pizza Fridays).

Meetings should be followed with something fun (e.g., a meeting and a hike, where people meet to discuss an event and then enjoy a hike). This increases attendance at the meeting (which helps distribute the workload) and creates social space for people to get to know each other and build community. Recognition activities are also a good way to create community (e.g., celebrating retirements, tenures, book publications, grants, Women's Day, May Day). These opportunities bring people together to celebrate one another, build community, and connect these moments with the fight for a better tomorrow. Our collective consciousness from resisting together is key to winning the larger fight against capitalism.

CONCLUSIONS, CHALLENGES, AND THE PERSISTENCE OF HOPE

People in Puerto Rico face the effects of debt repayment in every aspect of their lives. Therefore, one of the biggest organizing challenges is the fatigue of the few and the apathy of the many. Every time the crisis intensifies, there are so many fronts to cover that people get exhausted and frustrated. Those who lead the efforts burn out and often feel alone in the struggle. The people in the movement become overwhelmed and immobility increases. We must find a balance where we can live and fight without draining ourselves.

The renewal of leadership should be an organic sharing of the work. Delegating and asking others for help not only relieves your burden but also builds leadership skills. People work better when they feel useful and needed. Thus, we need to keep organizing, even when the attendance is low, even when people are not reacting like they should. Do not despair. The seeds we are planting will grow into a powerful movement, even if we might not see results right away. Every powerful movement needs some cooking time.

We are not alone in our struggle. In the Sixth Declaration of the Selva Lacandona, the Zapatistas say to all the dignified and rebel people who resist and fight against injustice all over the world:

> As there is a neoliberal globalization, there is a globalization of rebellion. And it is not just the workers of the countryside and of the city who appear in this globalization of rebellion, but others also appear who are much persecuted and despised for the same reason, for not letting themselves be dominated. . . many other groups who exist all over the world but who we do not see until they shout '*ya basta*' [enough] of being despised, and they raise up, and then we see them, we hear them, and we learn from them. And then we see that all those groups of people are fighting against neoliberalism, against the capitalist globalization plan, and their struggle is for humanity.[24]

---

[24] Zapatista Army of National Liberation, "Sixth Declaration of the Selva Lacandona," *Enlace Zapatista*, 2005, https://enlacezapatista.

Our greatest challenge in the fight against the debt economy is to continue weaving our resistances together with others (beyond our campuses and our countries) who also fight against capitalism. We can be inspired by others in the struggle. The persistent "collective global we" makes us stronger and brings hope. The labor movement is growing in the United States, and something is brewing in public colleges and universities.

This book has called for action against the debt economy. We do not wish to make prescriptions but do include a diversity of tactics and strategies that will help public higher education communities start their fight. We are all fighting against the same monster despite our complex differences and diverse struggles. We seek to dismantle the debt economy to take down capitalism. This sounds like a utopia and an insurmountable task, but it does not have to be. We fight for a better future of hope, joy, peace, justice, and freedom. As Slavoj Zizek reminds us:

> In a proper revolutionary breakthrough, the utopian future is neither simply fully realized, present, nor simply evoked as a distant promise. . . it is rather as if, the utopian future is already at hand, just there to be grabbed. Revolution is not experienced as a present hardship we have to endure for the happiness and freedom of the future generations, but as

---

ezln.org.

the present hardship over which this future happiness and freedom already cast their shadow—in it, we ALREADY ARE FREE WHILE FIGHTING FOR FREEDOM, we ALREADY ARE HAPPY WHILE FIGHTING FOR HAPPINESS, no matter how difficult the circumstances.[25]

We must embrace what we are fighting for to make it real and possible. Fighting to end capitalism frees us from capitalism. In fighting against debt, we take back what we are owed. We know debt is the opposite of life: we know that "life in debt is unworthy and dehumanizing, always undeserved and illegitimate; that to transform any country we must return to the bodies, to their diversities of race, gender, and class, to propose new forms of dialogue and go from there to action."[26] This fight will not be quick nor simple; it will require us to put our bodies and beings in the line of fire. Patience is essential—we go slow to go far.

We—the very important collective *we*—want to conclude this last chapter with words of hope that summarize the collective intentions of this book. May we embrace the fight against debt with optimism. May our words encourage others to act with confidence in the construction of anticapitalist futures. May our colleges and universities serve

---

[25] Slavoj Zizek, *Repeating Lenin*, (Zagreb: Arkzin, 2001).

[26] Ariadna Godreau, *Las Propias: Apuntes para una pedagogía de las endeudadas* (Toa Baja: Editora Educación Emergente, 2018), 58.

as sites of resistance, empowerment, and promise. May we lead with hope as we organize our anger to transform the places we inhabit within and beyond the university.

APPENDIX A
INFORMATION ON OUR
INSTITUTIONAL RATINGS
DATA SET

In Chapter 2, we presented some overarching results of original data analysis that allowed us to trace the inequities associated with debt financing in US higher education. There is more analysis to be done, both on the national and regional levels and at our individual institutions. What follows is a short introduction to the kinds of analysis possible using publicly available data.

We connected two datasets: (1) decades of data from the Integrated Postsecondary Education Data System (IPEDS), a government survey that gathers information on colleges that participate in federal financial aid programs, and (2) publicly available credit ratings from credit rating agencies. Putting the two together for over a thousand colleges and universities allowed us to trace the relationship between credit ratings and institutional characteristics, from the percentage of students receiving Pell Grants at an institution to the makeup of the institution's workforce and size of its endowment.

There are valid concerns about the use of IPEDS data, and we want to acknowledge and address those concerns here. IPEDS data is self-reported. The surveys used to collect IPEDS data center first-time, full-time, degree-seeking undergraduates. This poses a particular concern at a time when part-time, continuing, and online student populations are on the rise[1]; those student groups may be underrepresented in IPEDS data. Reporting errors can only be corrected for a year after submission, then data is permanently "locked."[2] The surveys and fields on them change over time, making long-term year-over-year data sometimes difficult to reliably analyze. The instructions provided to colleges and universities for how to calculate fields also change over time, and the workers in institutional research offices who fill out the surveys can make human errors. Nevertheless, IPEDS remains the broadest and most consistent reporting system for US higher education data.

The data set analyzed here consists of 752 rated issuers representing 1,109 nonprofit institutions. While private institutions are included in the data set, most of the analysis included only includes public institutions. Some issuers have a 1:1 relationship with an institution, and others issue debt on behalf of a number of universities (for instance, the Board

[1] Matt Zalaznick, "Student Demographics: Big Changes Are Forcing Reinvention on Campus," University Business, November 7, 2022, https://universitybusiness.com.

[2] NCES, "Timing of IPEDS Data Collection, Coverage, and Release Cycle," National Center for Education Statistics, n.d., https://nces.ed.gov.

of Regents of the Texas A&M University System represents eleven institutions). For college and university systems with a main campus and related branch campuses, the data from the main campus was used. For systems with multiple campuses and no "main" campus, the data from all institutions was used. For simplicity, we only used institutions' issuer ratings. Ratings are also given to specific bond issues (and may be influenced by the terms of that specific bond). The vast majority of publicly rated institutions are nonprime investment grade.

The 1,109 institutions in this data were divided into six cohorts by credit rating (using terms and divisions common in studies of credit ratings). Four cohorts are investment grade and two are speculative grade (also called high-yield, noninvestment grade, or junk, depending on the source). At some points in the analysis, cohorts were further combined into just "investment grade" and "speculative grade" for simplicity. More details on the cohorts can be found in the table below. When institutions had conflicting credit ratings, we used the highest credit rating. For the vast majority of institutions rated by more than one agency, the ratings fell into the same cohort band.

We chose to group institutions into cohorts by credit rating because these ratings directly impact the costs of financing.[3] Higher-rated institutions

---

[3] Jess Cornaggia, Kimberly Rodgers Cornaggia, and Ryan D. Israelsen, "Credit Ratings and the Cost of Municipal Financing," *Review of Financial Studies* 31, no. 6 (2018): 2038–79.

encounter lower costs to enter the bond market and are allowed to pay lower interest rates. Lower-rated institutions pay more to access the same funding streams. Leveraging credit ratings for analysis allows us to highlight what is valued and incentivized by the private sector. Credit ratings are used as a proxy for dividing institutions into cohorts by the interest or yield rates they must pay on their debt.

Credit rating cohorts as used for analysis within this chapter			
Credit Rating Cohort	Credit ratings of institutions in cohort (S&P or Fitch/Moody's)[4]	Number of institutions in cohort	FTE Fall 2021 Student Enrollment (DRVEF2021)
Investment Grade – Prime	AAA/Aaa	51	727,756
Investment Grade – High Grade	AA/Aa	479	5,158,994
Investment Grade – Upper Medium Grade	A/A	320	1,859,324
Investment Grade – Lower Medium Grade	BBB/Baa	193	560,565
Speculative – Non-investment Grade	BB/Ba	49	145,841
Speculative – Highly Speculative/ Substantial Risk/ Highly Vulnerable	B, CCC, CC/B, Caa, Ca	17	53,519

---

[4] Included in each cohort are the variations (aka notches, as they are called by the rating agencies) within these ratings. For instance, AA/Aa means all of the following ratings: AA-, AA, AA+, Aa3, Aa2, Aa1.

SOME OF OUR KEY FINDINGS

How do institutions with different credit ratings vary from one another? Highly rated institutions tend to be wealthier, whiter, and more affluent. Their primary function has shifted from education to finance. They have large endowments, whose investment returns make up a significant segment of institutional revenues. The "margins" (called "profit margins" outside of the nominally nonprofit world) of highly rated institutions are higher than those of many corporations. In order to make the most money possible, as well as to maintain a high rating or valuation, these profits are not reinvested in campuses or the students and workers who make them what they are. Profits are instead used to purchase more investments, to move further into the realm of finance and away from institutions' educational missions.

- Higher-rated institutions have more white students and fewer Black and Brown students than lower-rated institutions. In 2021, "investment grade" rated institutions averaged 8.6 percent Black or African American students, 12.9 percent Hispanic students, and 48.9 percent white students. Colleges and universities rated "speculative grade" had 13 percent Black or African American students, 32.39 percent Hispanic students, and 34 percent white students. In other words, lower-rated institutions had 52 percent more Black students, 151 percent more Hispanic students, and 30 percent fewer white students than higher-rated institutions.[5]

- The percentage of students receiving Pell Grants at an institution (a common analytical proxy for low-income students) is inversely related to the institution's credit rating. In other words, lower-income students make up less of the student population at highly-rated institutions. At the highest-rated public colleges and universities—those with prime or AAA/Aaa ratings—only 29.1 percent of students were awarded Pell Grants. At the lowest-rated public universities—those rated B and lower—a full 76.4 percent of students received this form of grant-based aid.[6]

- Prime-rated public institutions' endowments (or intergenerational institutional wealth) are 186 times larger per student than the lowest-rated institutions. At the lowest-rated public institutions, endowment holdings averaged just $492 per FTE student in 2021. The highest-rated public universities had $91,800 per FTE student in their endowments.[7]

---

[5] This analysis uses variables from the IPEDS "EF2021A All students total" table.

[6] This analysis uses variables from the IPEDS "DRVEF2021" (enrollment) and "SFA2021" (financial aid, including Pell Grants) tables.

[7] This analysis uses variables from the IPEDS "DRVEF2021" (enrollment) and "F2021_F1A" (public institution financial reporting) tables.

- Revenues at prime-rated public institutions—$91,261 per FTE student in 2021—overshadow the lowest-rated public institutions, which stood at $28,892 per FTE student.[8]
- At prime-rated public institutions, 28.55 percent of revenues in FY2021 came from investment income. At speculative-grade public institutions, only 0.22 percent of revenues came from investment income.[9]
- Traditionally, profits are calculated as revenues minus expenses. When we do this calculation for rated public institutions, we see a stark trend across credit rating grades: the higher the rating, the higher the ("nonprofit") profit margin. Prime-rated public institutions average a 31.3 percent profit margin. Speculative-grade public institutions have almost no profit margin at all (under 1 percent).[10]
- At prime-rated public institutions, nearly 11 percent of FTE staff were in business and financial operations. At the lowest-rated

---

[8] This analysis uses variables from the IPEDS "DRVEF2021" (enrollment) and "F2021_F1A" (public institution financial reporting) tables.

[9] This analysis uses variables from the IPEDS "F2021_F1A" (public institution financial reporting) table.

[10] This analysis uses variables from the IPEDS "DRVEF2021" (enrollment) and "F2021_F1A" (public institution financial reporting) tables.

public institutions, 3 percent of FTE workers were in business and financial operations.[11]

- Higher-rated institutions have significantly increased the percentage of their FTE staff dedicated to business and finance over the decade (2012–2021). Highly rated institutions also have a smaller proportion of workers dedicated to instruction, research, and public service, and fewer FTE staff dedicated to libraries and student and academic services.[12]

---

[11] This analysis uses variables from the IPEDS "DRVHR2021" (human resources) table.

[12] This analysis uses variables on salary and human resources data over time, namely the following tables: "SAL2012_NIS_RV" (2012), "SAL2013_NIS_RV" (2013), "SAL2014_NIS_RV" (2014), "SAL2015_ NIS_RV" (2015), "SAL2016_NIS_RV" (2016), "SAL2017_NIS_RV" (2017), "SAL2018_NIS_RV" (2018), "SAL2019_NIS_RV" (2019), "SAL2020_NIS_RV" (2020), and "SAL2021_NIS" (2021).

APPENDIX B
ORGANIZING A DEBT REVEAL ON YOUR CAMPUS

A debt reveal empowers faculty, staff, librarians, students, and community members to better understand their university's debt and its effects. They can then use this information to organize for a better public university. Encourage your collaborators to see this as a limited and achievable project tied to short and longer-term actions. There is no need for an intimidating (even demobilizing) comprehensive, detailed analysis of debt—that can come later if needed.

A debt reveal requires a small group of people, as few as two or as many as eight or nine. If you have difficulty recruiting comrades or students to join the effort, you may find the guidance in Chapter 3 particularly helpful. The pitch to build a team can be straightforward and nontechnical:

One of the lesser-known effects of long-term cuts in state funding for public higher education is that more and more campuses, as opposed to the state government, must pay for their dorms and academic buildings. This forces them to borrow money. The costs of this debt are passed on to students in the form of higher tuition and fees. In many schools, each full-time undergrad pays about $2,500 toward debt servicing annually. This has many consequences. It pulls money away from educational purposes and thus undermines the quality of the education. It increasingly requires that the board/trustees/regents prioritize creditworthiness over educational goals. It also undermines the idea that public higher education should be a public good. We are forming a team to start looking into campus debt and its implications for our school.

Even more succinctly: "Find out how much debt our campus has, what it is for, and how it affects education at XXX university!" You do not need any economics or financial specialists. In fact, having people from different fields and experiences can both broaden and deepen the analysis and demonstrate that all campus members can and should understand university finances.

GATHERING INFORMATION

This is an organizing project, not a research project. Focus on key information that is accessible in online public documents and sources. Most public documents are searchable, making research easier once you know a few key terms.

The first step is to learn how borrowing works on your campus. We recommend obtaining the most recent annual financial statement for your university (it may also be called a financial report or independent audit or be embedded in the university's annual report). In some states, university financial statements are prepared at the system level (e.g., SUNY), not the campus level. A simple online search for the most recent university financial statement should work, but if that fails, you can write to your university public records officer, chief financial officer, or governing board administrator. Many states have laws that require public records requests to be fulfilled within a set time.

Once you locate the most recent statement, search for instances of the word "bond." Most bond information will be located in the "Long-Term Liabilities" section of the audit. You should now be able to determine whether:

- Your university has independent bonding (borrowing) authority (i.e., the university is the issuer/borrower of the bonds and is directly responsible for paying the debt service). For example, Oregon State University's financial statements[1] show that the university issues bonds directly. This is called on-book debt.
- Borrowing goes through a quasi-public building authority/corporation established by the state. This authority is the issuer and charges

---

[1] University of Oregon, "2021 Annual Financial Report," University of Oregon, n.d., https://pages.uoregon.edu.

your campus debt service or requires that debt service is built into student fees. This may show up as "off-book debt." For example, the Salem State University audit shows that borrowing goes through the Massachusetts State College Building Authority.

- Borrowing is done by a component of your university, such as a non-profit corporation or a university foundation (i.e., the component unit is the issuer, and the campus pays them rent or transfers funds regularly). For example, the University of Tennessee (UT) financial statements[2] show that the University of Tennessee Foundation borrows for capital projects that improve UT, and the university transfers about $30 million annually to the UT foundation.

It could also be some combination of the above.[3]

Once you know the name(s) of the bonding issuer (the lender) involved, start collecting information about them (if it is not your campus itself). In the case of public building authorities and

---

[2] The University of Tennessee, "Annual Financial Report 2020," The University of Tennessee, n.d., https://treasurer.tennessee.edu.

[3] There are other financing schemes that we do not address in this reveal guide (e.g., lines of credit and partnering with a private corporation in a public-private partnership, or P3). Furthermore, some borrowing for campus projects is done and paid for by the state. The reveal is limited to the debt that universities (and students) are on the hook for.

corporations, federal law requires that they also publish annual financial statements/audits. These are usually easy to find online by searching for the organization's full name.

Another excellent place to look is the EMMA (Electronic Municipal Market Access) municipal bond website.[4] On the main page, select your state to start the search and then use the textbox to search for the names of the bonding issuer(s). Once located, there are tabs for "Official Statements" and links to the most recent bond statement issued (top of the list). These documents are long and technical. You don't have to read through the whole thing. Rather, focus on the sections that concern debt service payments and payment schedules.

With your university's financial statement, relevant bond statements, and building authority documents in hand, you are ready to uncover campus debt! We provide guidance below and additional digital resources on "The *Other* College Debt Crisis"[5] website. This includes a debt audit worksheet[6] to simplify the calculations. *The worksheet will automatically do all the calculations discussed below. All you have to do is enter the data!*

A few words of warning: sometimes being too detailed can be detrimental. You don't want an

---

[4] Electronic Municipal Market Access: https://emma.msrb.org/.

[5] The *Other* College Debt Crisis: https://salemmscadocs.home.blog/.

[6] Worksheet with Salem State example: https://salemmscadocs.home.blog/debt-audit-tool-kit/ and click on "Download" debtrevealworksheet-4.

opponent saying, "Your figures are off by two cents, so how can we rely on any of your data?" Never exaggerate your data. Whenever there is the slightest doubt, present your figures in a way that understates your claim. You can choose the lower end of a range or simply state, "Average per capita student capital debt on campus is about $2,500." That way, you cannot be accused of exaggerating the problem.

CALCULATING YOUR CAMPUS' DEBT BURDEN

It can be provocative to report the total indebtedness of your university. Information about this can be found in the university's financial statement; look at the section on long-term liabilities and find the total amount due for "bonds payable." You can add in lease liabilities too, especially if these are twenty-plus-year lease agreements with building authorities or corporations. Note that there may be other "off-book" debt not captured in the university financial statement.

The next analysis considers whether campus debt is straining your university finances.[7] Begin

---

[7] In some states, like New York, capital borrowing is exclusively handled and paid for by state agencies and building authorities. Hence, there is no debt service obligation impacting the public university budgets. However, auxiliary facilities in these states are independently financed using pledged student revenue, so the cost of debt service to students still can and should be revealed. In such cases, it is critical to obtain the building authority's most recent

by finding how much your university is paying in debt service annually. This information may be spelled out in your university's financial statement—search for "debt service," "debt payments," or "long-term debt" to find the amount paid for debt service in that fiscal year.[8] If your university doesn't borrow directly, this information might not be reported (as it is considered "off-book" debt).[9] This process can help judge how transparent your university is regarding campus-related debt! While looking at the university's financial statement, jot down the university's total annual operating revenue and enter it in line 7 of the worksheet. Look through the other documents that you gathered to further record the debt payments your university or university system has pledged to pay annually. Search for payment schedules using different combinations of terms like "debt service," "schedule," "requirements," "payment," and "pledge."[10] Enter the debt service in line 8 of the worksheet.

---

annual report and bond issuance to calculate the proportion of auxiliary student fees that are used to service debt.

[8] Many universities restructured their loans in FY2021 to reduce their debt service during the pandemic. Check the debt service payments over a number of years to ensure you are not relying on an artificially low debt service figure.

[9] See our "Seeking Information on Debt and Debt Service" (http://tinyurl.com/yc26c4t3) instructions for more information on finding off-book debt.

[10] If you are using a building authority financial statement, payments owed by universities may be termed "pledged revenues" or "schedule of revenues."

214 | LEND & RULE

To calculate your campus' yearly debt burden ratio, divide the annual debt service amount by the university's total operating revenue. At Salem State, the university paid $17,912,083 in debt service. This number divided by the campus' operating revenue ($175,842,757), yields a debt burden ratio of 10.19 percent (line 14).

Most university boards set a debt burden threshold that cannot be exceeded (about 5–10 percent). These can frequently be found by searching for the university's name and "debt policy." The average debt ratio threshold set for public universities is 7 percent. However, a report by EY Parthenon (2021),[11] a higher education financial consulting firm employed under the Baker Administration in Massachusetts, warns that maxing out on debt capacity is problematic for institutions with low growth or decline. Instead of advising public campus leaders to demand more public funding for their campuses, the Parthenon report suggests that campuses burdened with debt enter into "public-private partnerships to monetize campus assets" or to serve their missions better by sharing resources with other colleges, including through "mergers and acquisition." This advice reinforces the neoliberal paradigm and accelerates the next phase of eliminating public higher education as a public good, namely public-private partnerships.

---

[11] EY Parthenon, "How Higher Education Institutions Can Best Leverage Debt as a Strategic Tool," Ernst & Young LLP, n.d., https://assets.ey.com.

CALCULATING COSTS TO STUDENTS

Inevitably students pay the cost of their university's debt. If your campus financial statements are truly transparent, they may publish the annual cost to students for debt service, as Salem State did.[12] If not, it's easy to figure out using the worksheet.

Calculate the per-student cost by dividing the annual debt service payment by the number of full-time equivalent (FTE) students at your university. This FTE number can be obtained using the IPEDS (Integrated Postsecondary Education Data System) data tool.[13] Use the "Look up an Institution" tool and select the "Enrollment" tab. In FY2020, Salem State paid $17,912,083 in debt service and had 5,402 FTE undergraduate students. Enter this number on line 17 of the worksheet. This means that the average debt service cost to students was $3,316 (line 18). In other words, if the campus was not borrowing to cover the cost of dorms and other campus facilities, students would pay about three thousand dollars less in yearly fees! Importantly, this is only an average—residential students pay sub-stantially more debt-related fees than commuters.

You will need to decide whether or not to include graduate students in your calculations of FTEs. At Salem State University, the graduate programs are offered at night and online, so grad students are

---

[12] Salem State University, "Ratio Calculations & Other Measure-ments," Salem State University, June 30, 2019: 6.

[13] Click "Look up an Institution" at: https://nces.ed.gov/ipeds/use-the-data.

not charged fees for the debt-financed campus aux-iliary services (except for parking). Therefore, we opted to only use the undergraduate FTE number. However, if your university has a large percentage of graduate students—especially if they live in uni-versity housing—you may want to include them in the calculation.

Students are often shocked to learn how much of their tuition and fees goes to debt servicing. *This percentage can be calculated by dividing the uni-versity's annual debt service payment by its annual revenue generated from tuition and fees* (line 22). The tuition and fee figures can be found in the uni-versity's financial statement under the section for "operating revenue." Add student revenue from auxiliary services to the reported *net* tuition and fee number (which removes scholarships). In FY2020, Salem State paid $17,912,083 in debt service. The student net fee revenue was $65,755,308 and the auxiliary service revenue was $24,082,551 for a total of $89,837,859. Therefore, nearly 20 percent of student fee payments went to service the univer-sity's debt (line 22).

Students will also be surprised to learn how campus debt affects student debt. With the cal-culated per-student debt service cost above (line 18), *you can illustrate how much student loan totals could be reduced if university debt was abolished. For a conservative estimate, we suggest multiplying the per-student cost by four years (knowing many students take more than four years to complete their degree).* At Salem State, if there was no campus debt, the average undergraduate's student loan total could be reduced by at least $13,263 (more for students who take longer than four years).

CALCULATING INSTRUCTIONAL HARM

This analysis helps you operationalize the "instructional harm" of debt. In other words, what instructional elements have been sacrificed to service debt? The idea is that funds for servicing debt could otherwise be used to reduce tuition and fees or pay for critical services (e.g., hiring more faculty, increasing student services), or a combination of both.

First, *calculate how many more full-time faculty could be hired and/or part-time faculty lines converted to full-time by dividing the annual debt service by the average FT faculty salary + fringe benefits (line 28).* If your school does not publish this data, you can look for the mean FT faculty salary (line 25) on the IPEDS website.[14] For average benefit rates (line 26), consult the Bureau of Labor Statistics website, which reports the average *employer costs for employee compensation* for state and local employees in the 'education—college and university' subgroup.[15] In

---

[14] Click "Look up an Institution" at: https://nces.ed.gov/ipeds/use-the-data; IPEDS does not provide salary information for every year.

[15] This figure—which is calculated by dividing the percent of total compensation that goes to total benefits by the percent of total compensation that goes to wages and salaries—is updated in reports on the Bureau of Labor Statistics' website regularly. Search for "Employer Costs for Employee Compensation."

2020, the benefits-to-salary ratio was 55.7 percent for this subgroup. You can now calculate the average salary and fringe benefits per FT instructor: average salary plus the average salary multiplied by the fringe benefit rate (line 27). Then, divide the annual debt payment by this figure to obtain the number of FT faculty positions that the annual debt payment could support.

The second calculation illustrates *how many more course sections could be added in a year if there was no campus debt (line 31). Multiply the figure above for the number of new FT positions by the average number of courses a full-time faculty member teaches* (as part of their workload) at your university (line 30). You can get this figure either from the union contract or through discussions with faculty (a handy way to involve members!).

In addition to these different representations of instructional harm, we suggest you start conversations on campus with open-ended questions that allow you to highlight other ways debt service burden harms your university:

> What are some examples of recent cuts to academic programs and student services (e.g., counseling, advising, financial aid services) that happened because of budget constraints?
>
> Are there enough faculty, librarians, and staff to serve the mission of the university?
>
> What campus capital improvements are being postponed due to a lack of money?
>
> How would the student experience be different if tuition and fees were not so high?

REVEALING FOR CHANGE

As this generally opaque information is transformed into real-life impacts for students and higher education workers, it will hopefully make the costs of institutional debt clearer and help to organize people in the fight against it and for a fully funded, more democratic, antiracist public higher education. Your fellow workers and students will not want to process a long report on campus debt. It is better to prepare eye-catching infographics to display the campus debt problem.[16]

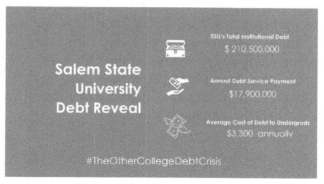

Debt Reveal infographic from Salem State University.

You can showcase your campus debt findings on flyers, in campus publications, and on social media. A campus debt reveal event can also be powerful. It can be as simple as hosting a Zoom gathering in which you share and discuss the data. You

---

[16] We chose to display ballpark, rounded numbers in media reports to avoid campus administration quibbling over exact figures, which can vary slightly, depending on which source you rely on.

could also set up a table in the middle of campus to collect signatures for a petition against students paying for their college's debt. You might also write a local media press release about your debt findings or reveal event.[17]

Remember, campus debt work is not standalone work *per se*. We need to integrate debt work into other union and even non-union campus organizing work. For example, integrate campus debt analysis into your union's analysis of the campus budget and legislative action work, your campus' strategic plan or vision (including analysis of proposals for downsizing, layoffs, etc.), the accreditation process, making old and new buildings safe and green, and contract demands. This way, you avoid asking people to take on the additional work of joining your efforts to expose campus debt. Rather, you can use knowledge of campus debt to *expand* their ongoing work.

---

[17] See a sample in the digital toolkit at www.TheOtherCollegeDebt-Crisis.org.

GLOSSARY

Auxiliary services: The auxiliary services are non-educational services that create income/profit for the university. They can be directly run by the university or subcontracted out. Auxiliary services include but are not limited to, campus housing, dining/meal services, parking (garages), and campus bookstores.

Bonds: For our purposes, a bond is a loan that a university or, in some cases, the state government, receives from an investor (the debtholder or creditor). "To issue a bond" means asking creditors to lend you money. Not all institutions can directly issue bonds; some have to go through state or municipal governments. Bonds usually have a set rate of interest paid to the creditor (in public bonds, usually a fixed rather than a variable rate) and a specified end date by which the principal is due to be paid in full. Owners of the bonds have certain rights, including first access to resources to guarantee repayment of the loan and either collateral or the 'good faith' of the state government.

Debt service: The amount paid towards the bond obligation, including principal and interest, and any amount that might be assessed to meet debt service reserve fund requirements. The annual debt service is the payment due each year, while total debt service is the full amount to be repaid.

Fringe Benefit Rate: Fringe benefits are the additional benefits that an employee receives above their salary. The fringe benefit rate is the *employer's total contribution* to these benefits over the total salary, including Social Security and Medicare taxes, unemployment and workers comp, and sometimes disability insurance, health insurance, life insurance, pension contribution, and paid leave. In recent years, many state governments have transferred an increasing portion of fringe benefits costs from the state to individual universities. The proportion of the overall fringe benefits that a given university pays varies from state to state (and may vary within states) based on various factors. *Our worksheet uses the highest and most inclusive fringe benefit rate, even though most universities do not pay this rate. This means that our calculation of full-time academic positions lost to debt service (line 28) is an absolute minimum.*

On-book/off-book debt (also known as on-ledger/off-ledger debt): Any loan taken directly by the university is on-book (or on-ledger). However, if a loan is taken by a larger state agency (a state building authority), it is an off-ledger debt for the university (though they are still obligated to repay the loan in full). As noted in the worksheet, the general guideline for on-ledger debt is 5 percent and for total debt (including off-ledger debt) is 10 percent. Off-ledger debt is usually reported in the annual audit.

Operating Revenues/Expenses: The revenue that an institution generates from its educational activities, including net tuition and fees, federal, state, and private grants, and contracts, sales, and services from educational departments. This excludes general state appropriations, investments, and interest. Operating expenses include educational expenses and expenses for auxiliary enterprises.

ABOUT THE AUTHORS

Coalition Against Campus Debt is a collective of educators and organizers active in higher education struggles as well as the debt abolition movement more widely for over a decade. Members include Jason Thomas Wozniak, Eleni Schirmer, Dana Morrison, Joanna Gonsalves, Richard Levy, María del Mar Rosa-Rodríguez, Sofya Aptekar, Tracy Berger, and Barbara Madeloni.

* * *

Sofya Aptekar is an associate professor of urban studies at the City University of New York School of Labor and Urban Studies. She is the author of *Green Card Soldier* (MIT, 2023) and a delegate of the Professional Staff Congress.

Tracy Berger is a mom of two, member of United Campus Workers Colorado, and staff organizer with Higher Education Labor United (HELU). She previously worked as staff at the University of Colorado Boulder and Front Range Community College.

María del Mar Rosa-Rodríguez is an associate professor of Hispanic Studies at the University of Puerto Rico at Cayey, and the president of the faculty union of the UPR, Asociación Puertorriqueña de Profesores Universitarios (APPU). She is also the cofounder of the Junte de Mujeres Sindicalistas, bringing together feminism and syndicalism.

Joanna Gonsalves is a psychology professor at Salem State University and president of the Massachusetts State College Association faculty union.

Rich Levy is a professor of Political Science emeritus at Salem State University and a member of Educators for a Democratic Union. He and Joanna Gonsalves are coordinators of the Massachusetts Campus Debt Reveal and the Massachusetts Anti-Privatization Project, both funded by the Massachusetts Teachers Association.

Barbara Madeloni is an organizer and writer for *Labor Notes*.

Dana Morrison is an associate professor in the Educational Foundations and Policy Studies Department at West Chester University of Pennsylvania and chapter secretary of the Association of Pennsylvania State College and University Faculties.

Eleni Schirmer is a writer living in Montreal. She organizes with the Debt Collective.

Jason Thomas Wozniak is an associate professor in the Educational Foundations and Policy Studies Department, coordinator of the Transformative

Education and Social Change Program, and co-director of the Latin American Philosophy of Education Society (LAPES) at West Chester University. He is also a long-term organizer with the Debt Collective.

ABOUT COMMON NOTIONS

Common Notions is a publishing house and programming platform that fosters new formulations of living autonomy. We aim to circulate timely reflections, clear critiques, and inspiring strategies that amplify movements for social justice.

Our publications trace a constellation of critical and visionary meditations on the organization of freedom. By any media necessary, we seek to nourish the imagination and generalize common notions about the creation of other worlds beyond state and capital. Inspired by various traditions of autonomism and liberation—in the US and internationally, historical and emerging from contemporary movements—our publications provide resources for a collective reading of struggles past, present, and to come.

Common Notions regularly collaborates with political collectives, militant authors, radical presses, and maverick designers around the world. Our political and aesthetic pursuits are dreamed and realized with Antumbra Designs.

www.commonnotions.org
info@commonnotions.org

BECOME A COMMON NOTIONS MONTHLY SUSTAINER

These are decisive times ripe with challenges and possibility, heartache, and beautiful inspiration. More than ever, we need timely reflections, clear critiques, and inspiring strategies that can help movements for social justice grow and transform society.

Help us amplify those words, deeds, and dreams that our liberation movements, and our worlds, so urgently need.

Movements are sustained by people like you, whose fugitive words, deeds, and dreams bend against the world of domination and exploitation.

For collective imagination, dedicated practices of love and study, and organized acts of freedom.
By any media necessary.
With your love and support.

Monthly sustainers start at $15 and receive each new book in our publishing program.

commonnotions.org/sustain

MORE FROM COMMON NOTIONS

New York Liberation School
Study and Movement for the People's
University

Connor Tomás Reed

978-1-942173-68-7
Paperback | 256 pages | 6 x 9 in | $22
Education | Archive | Feminism

In the 1960s and '70s—when Toni Cade
Bambara, Samuel Delany, David Hender-
son, June Jordan, Audre Lorde, Guillermo
Morales, Adrienne Rich, and Assata Shakur
all studied and taught at CUNY—New York City's classrooms and
streets radiated as epicenters of Black, Puerto Rican, queer, and women's
liberation. Highlighting the decolonial feminist metamorphosis that
transformed our educational landscape, New York Liberation School ex-
plores how study and movement coalesced across classrooms and neigh-
borhoods.

Wages for Students

George Caffentzis, Monty Neill, and
John Willshire-Carrera

978-1-942173-02-1
Paperback | 224 pages | 4.5 x 6 in | $13.95
Education | Archive | Social Movements

Wages for Students was published anony-
mously as "a pamphlet in the form of
a blue book" by activists linked to the
journal *Zerowork* during student strikes
in Massachusetts and New York in the fall
of 1975. Deeply influenced by the Wages for Housework Campaign's
analysis of capitalism, and relating to struggles such as Black Power,
anticolonial resistance, and the antiwar movements, the authors fought
against the role of universities as conceived by capital and its state. The
pamphlet debates the strategies of the student movement at the time
and denounces the regime of forced unpaid work imposed every day
upon millions of students.